CULTURE SHOCK!

USA

Esther Wanning

29 August '04

To Lady & Aldwin,

A token of our
appreciation to
your ministry
in IPC —
and hopefully
this book helps
you in your
new home.

The IPC folks

TIMES BOOKS INTERNATIONAL

In the same series

Argentina	Ecuador	Korea	South Africa
Australia	Egypt	Laos	Spain
Austria	Finland	Malaysia	Sri Lanka
Belgium	France	Mauritius	Sweden
Bolivia	Germany	Mexico	Switzerland
Borneo	Greece	Morocco	Syria
Brazil	Hong Kong	Myanmar	Taiwan
Britain	Hungary	Nepal	Thailand
California	India	Netherlands	Turkey
Canada	Indonesia	Norway	UAE
Chile	Iran	Pakistan	Ukraine
China	Ireland	Philippines	USA
Costa Rica	Israel	Saudi Arabia	USA—The South
Cuba	Italy	Scotland	Venezuela
Czech Republic	Japan	Singapore	Vietnam
Denmark			

Living & Working Abroad series

Barcelona	Munich
Beijing	New York
Chicago	Paris
Havana	Rome
Jakarta	San Francisco
Kuala Lumpur	Shanghai
London	Tokyo
Moscow	Vancouver

Other books in the series

A Globe-Trotter's Guide	Living & Working Abroad
A Parent's Guide	Personal Protection
A Student's Guide	At Home and Abroad
A Traveller's Medical Guide	Working Holidays Abroad
A Wife's Guide	

Illustrations by TRIGG
Cover photographs by Esther Wanning

© 1991 Esther Wanning
© 2000 Times Media Private Limited
Revised 1997, 1999, 2003
Reprinted 1993, 1995, 1996, 2000, 2003

Published by Times Books International
an imprint of Times Media Pte Ltd
Times Centre, 1 New Industrial Road, Singapore 536196
Tel: (65) 62139288 Fax: (65) 62854871 Email: te@tpl.com.sg
Online Bookstore: www.timesone.com.sg/te

Times Subang
Lot 46, Subang Hi-Tech Industrial Park, Batu Tiga, 40000 Shah Alam,
Selangor Darul Ehsan, Malaysia
Tel & Fax: (603) 56363517 Email: cchong@tpg.com.my

Printed in Singapore
ISBN 981 232 739 8

To Barbara Creaturo,
who made an author out of me.

National Library Board (Singapore) Cataloguing in Publication Data

Wanning, Esther.
Culture shock! :- USA /- Esther Wanning. – Singapore :-
Times Books International,- 2003. p. cm.
– (Culture shock!)

ISBN : 981-232-739-8
1. Etiquette – United States. 2. United States- – Social life and customs.
I. Title. II. Series: Culture shock!

E161   973 — dc21   SLS2003027379

CONTENTS

The Family 59

Daily Life 84

God and Country 118

Education 125

FOREWORD

Any book that attempts to generalise about culture must begin with a disclaimer. No amount of research frees a writer from her own particular background. This is mine, which undoubtedly affects my outlook: I'm a native of the state of Massachusetts, which makes me a "Yankee." My forebears were mainly Scottish, English, Irish, and Dutch. I spent part of my childhood in a small farming town in New York State's Hudson River Valley and treasured this experience of small-town life in a place that clung to old-fashioned American values. As an adult, I lived for a dozen years in New York City and have spent the last 27 years in California, where I married into a Jewish family of Hungarian and Eastern European origins.

I have my grandmother, Mary Hannah Augusta Fife Emerson, to thank for early instruction in correct behaviour. Her emphasis on points of etiquette left me more observant of the lapses of others than I would sometimes wish to be.

However, the fish do not have the necessary perspective for reporting on their own sea, and this book could not have been written without the help of the many immigrants I interviewed, some of whom were old friends. Their reflections make up the backbone of this book. My greatest thanks go to Ali Awartani, An-Ching Chang, Uwe Dobers, Mufeed Droubi, Ocean Epstein, Angelo Garro, Brian Gitta, Bernadette Glenn, Greg Gorel, Agneta Heijl, Lakshmi Karna, Lata Karna, Fauz Kassamali, Dorothy Kino, Fusao Kiuchi, Ashis Mukhopadhyay, Citania Tam, Mike Pham, Edda Piccini, Elizabeth and Marian Price, Alice Leong Smith, and Regina Waldman.

Kathleen Wolf directed me to some rare texts (such as Judy Winn-Bell Olsen's unpublished *Little Glimpses*) and also arranged for me to meet her language classes and those of Josephine Lewis at Alemany

Community College in San Francisco. For the second edition, she arranged for meetings with the classes at City College of San Francisco, who brought me a fresh and updated outlook. In all cases these roomfuls of students from around the world produced wonderful insights.

For editorial help, earnest thanks go to Andrews Wanning, Beth Gutcheon and Robin Clements, Suzanne Mantell, Jim Churchill, and Nikki Meredith. For other kinds of help, I am grateful to Kristy MacDonald, Sally Taylor, Patricia Emerson Watson, Rufus Wanning, Bill Wilson, Kathy Stein, Lynn Ferrin, and Elsa and Alfred Lipsey. For generosity with photographs, Marcia Lieberman and *The Weekly Packet* of Blue Hill, Maine. For hospitality above and beyond the call of duty, the Press family of California. For her good work and supportiveness, thanks are overdue to my agent, Heide Lange.

Finally, I must thank those many cultural analysts who went before me, whose books are listed in the bibliography at the end.

—Esther Wanning, 2003

INTRODUCTION

Foreign vacationers to the United States are likely to return home delighted by our country. The US's vastness and landscapes surpass expectation, the richness of ordinary homes seems astonishing, and above all, the friendliness of the people to strangers is unforgettable.

Culture shock is what happens when you stick around a little longer. It is the most natural – and elusive – of ailments. "If one were to offer men the choice of all the customs in the world, they would examine the whole number and end up by preferring their own," wrote the Greek historian Herodotus almost 25 centuries ago, describing culture shock. But we rarely are insightful enough to realise that it's cultural differences that separate us. We don't see our own ways of doing things as conditioned in the cradle. We see them as correct, and we conclude that the people from the other country have grave failings.

So our longer-term visitors start to complain: "These Americans are always in a hurry; they are so materialistic; they aren't sincere; the children are spoiled; they don't care about their families." The points vary according to country of origin. Brazilians find us work-crazed, Japanese think we are self-indulgent, the Chinese think we're selfish, the British consider us unsophisticated, and the Mexicans call us greedy.

This book attempts to explain why we act the way we do, and in what ways our behaviour is in accordance with the cultural values. Some of these values may seem questionable to you, but if you grasp what makes Americans tick, your stay here – whether long or short – will be far more interesting and your culture shock shorter lasting. And perhaps you will be more forgiving of the aspects of American behaviour that trouble you.

If you have come to stay for good, it is all the more important that you try to be sympathetic to American culture. In fact, you will do best to acquire some American qualities yourself if you want to succeed. Furthermore, you don't want to end up in one of those enclaves of foreigners which nourish themselves on disdain for America – while their children are becoming more and more American. (This is not the same thing as valuing your own customs and culture, a blameless idea.)

"When in Rome, do as the Romans do" is a useful adage for both immigrants and short-term visitors, but to follow it you must know what they do. We often unconsciously judge others by behaviour that we aren't even conscious of noticing. For instance, if you offer a limp handshake to an American while looking downwards, the American will not imagine that you are behaving very politely by your own rules; instead he will assume that you are uninterested in meeting him. If you know what American customs are, you will find your encounters with Americans both more fruitful and more frequent.

Americans are straightforward, and yes means yes and no means no. Our protocol is not strict, and in social situations, you needn't be overly concerned about correct behaviour. If you eat with the wrong fork or wear blue jeans to a cocktail party, people are unlikely to be offended. There are few taboos, and little formality is expected of anyone.

However, although there's a lot of freedom, there are limits. After reading this book, you should know where those limits lie. Meanwhile, smile – as Americans constantly do – ask questions when you're puzzled and don't worry too much about behaviour. "In the end," an Indian friend said after enumerating her complaints about Americans, "people are really more alike than different." If you learn the native customs and even come to understand the natives, you will go beyond the small differences and on to the big things that we all have in common.

Chapter One

AMERICAN VALUES

Like peoples everywhere, Americans don't think of themselves as having American values. We simply imagine that the qualities we hold dear are those that matter to all mankind.

In this we are mistaken. American values are uncommon. This becomes clear when an American advisor launches a project in an underdeveloped country. The American, who plans to bring prosperity to the natives, ends up in despair because nothing gets done. He cannot imagine that there are societies where getting things done isn't top priority. He is baffled to discover people who do not seem to want to improve themselves. He cannot understand individuals who are not eager to change their status in society. He goes home in defeat, thanking God that he is an American.

What he does not understand is that American values could only have been forged in a new country full of opportunity. We are a nation almost entirely of immigrants, steeped in the belief that anyone with talent can get ahead. We cannot comprehend people who think it is more important to go visit a sick mother-in-law than to put in a new sewage system.

American culture is commonly dated from the first permanent English settlement of 1607; from that point we see our history as a record of progress: from wilderness to jet planes in a few centuries. We conquered the original inhabitants, overthrew the English rulers, cleared the forests, opened the West, built skyscrapers, won the World Wars and extended the comfortable life to the masses. We achieved all this – as we see it – because of dynamic individuals who never stopped seeking a better way.

This viewpoint may change in the 21st century. Certain realities are beginning to affect our sunny outlook towards the future: We no longer have the highest living standard in the world, and today's young people cannot assume that they'll be better off than their parents. The road to success looks more difficult than it did a generation ago. Terrorist attacks have made the world a scarier place. But our response at present remains to work harder, not to look for satisfaction elsewhere. Realities change much faster than values.

Equality

It is a sacred belief in America that all people should have an equal chance at success. Such an idea could only be taken so seriously in a nation of great opportunity, and it has been opportunity, as much as democracy, that has made America the "Land of the Free." Were resources scarce and possibilities limited, people would only be free to go nowhere, and equality would have had a very different meaning.

When the USA was founded, the population was small and the resources were vast; those both aggressive and lucky could go far.

In 1782, a Frenchman, St. John de Crevecoeur, noted that it was in going from a servant to a master that a man became an American. Actually, many people through the years remained downtrodden, but there have been enough examples of upward mobility to keep the myth of equality alive. Democracy could promise visible fruits. Everybody might not win, but everybody (so goes the myth) was eligible to get out on the racecourse. Family and connections were not required. Effort and brains and imagination were.

Because the country's natural resources seemed endless, Americans developed an economics of abundance. We do not see our personal wealth as having been gained at the expense of others. Instead, we think of the rich as creating opportunities and jobs for others. We are very frank about admiring rich people, and, despite recent scandals exposing executive dishonesty, we consider wealth a sign of merit.

The American system traditionally contributes the sense that everybody plays by the same rules. The government's job is to keep the course equal, to protect the rights of every aspirant. When people at least believe that they have a chance, it seems worthwhile to try to advance themselves – and when they fail, to try again. If, on the contrary, they feel that only those in favoured positions can succeed, they are not inspired to make an effort. Despite the fact that it obviously is not so, we like to think that anyone can become President of the United States – regardless of family, wealth, or background.

"Any man's son may become the equal of any other man's son," wrote Fanny Trollope on visiting the United States in 1831, "and the consciousness of this is certainly a spur to exertion."

Much as conditions have changed since 1607 – the frontier wasn't endless, industrial competition comes from around the world, and the greatest predictor of success is having successful parents – the conviction remains that each person is responsible for his or her own advancement. People who don't succeed tend to blame themselves, no matter how unlucky they may have been.

Future Outlook

Americans are profoundly future-oriented. Whereas other societies look to the past for guidance, we cast our nets forward. We have a nearly exclusive respect for the future and what it will bring, and it's this belief in a brighter future that has given Americans their optimism. Whereas most peoples aren't surprised by cycles of good times and bad, we are accustomed to looking at our history as a record of forward progress We trust that we have the power to affect the course of events. We do not believe that bad things are God's will, things to be endured.

Even these days, when statistics show the rich getting richer and the poor poorer – and when not all progress seems positive (environmental problems, job losses, community breakdown, etc.) – the belief remains that for every problem there is a rational solution. If it's ourselves we must change, we do so. Or perhaps it is all the government's fault.

The idea that life can always be improved accounts for Americans being in such a hurry. The contemplative man accepts the world as it is; the active man changes it. It is change that Americans believe in. Consequently, to say that somebody is "very energetic" (no matter in what cause) is one of our highest compliments.

Future Shock

Because change comes so thick and fast, the American has been called "the constantly jumping man." Recent decades have been particularly fast-paced, in gadgetry as well as in mores. In the last few years, home fax machines, cellular phones, internet access, Palm Pilots, DVDs, and a pill for dogs that sterilises fleas have become commonplace. Alvin Toffler in his popular 1970 book, *Future Shock,* made the claim that all Americans are living in a state of shock due to the increasing tempo of change in our lives. Future shock, he says, is worse than culture shock because there is no resolution. The only resource is to become more adaptable than ever before, leading to a loss of identity.

Photo: Marcia Lieberman

Children are encouraged to do things for themselves at a young age.

Independence

Cowboys never were a large part of the population, and they're very scarce now, but in many ways they characterise the American ideal – self-reliant, tough, risk-taking, and masculine. The cowboy stands alone, pitting himself against the elements. His strongest tie is to his horse.

In many countries, people cannot conceive of themselves apart from the family or group they belong to; their loyalty is to the group and their achievements are for the group. In America, instead, self-reliance is the fundamental virtue. Each person is a solo operation, and independence is considered the birthright of every child. Our highest aspiration is self-fulfilment, and it's only the unencumbered person who can become his true self. Many decisions that would be made by the family or group in other cultures are made by the individual here.

15

Newcomers, especially those from tightly knit families, are frequently surprised to discover that American children quite regularly leave home – with their parents' blessings – at the age of 18. From then on, they will make most of their own decisions without their parents' help, having already been quite independent during their teenage years. A grown child who doesn't leave home is a source of concern. The child's job is to go out into the world and succeed. The job of the parents is to give the children every opportunity while they are growing up and then get out of their way.

Realistically, there are many ways in which families can and do help their grown children, but they will try to make light of their assistance. Children are not to be burdened with a sense of obligation.

Asian families, who by working together often quickly become home owners in the United States, are surprised to discover that American parents are not expected to contribute to the down payment on a house for their married children. The expectation is that children can achieve success without their parents' help, and not helping them would also leave them free of obligation to their parents. However – especially in these times of high real estate prices – it leaves many of them unlikely to ever own a house.

Many of the aspects of American life that seem most baffling to foreigners make sense in light of the freedom principle. Aged parents as well as children remain independent. If you want to go to Belize and open a boarding house, you do. If you want to walk alone to the North Pole, go ahead. You will be admired for achieving your goals. You don't have to stay home to take care of your elders.

In fact, sticking around your home town could suggest a lack of backbone, a failure of imagination and courage. Psychologists like to see families in which each member is "differentiated" rather than "enmeshed." People who are enmeshed with their families can't break away to follow their dreams. The majority of foreigners look "enmeshed" to American psychologists. To us, the individual comes first. We do not consider this selfish. A person serves society by living up to his potential. The classic American hero is someone who succeeds on his own, pulling himself up by his own bootstraps. The finest American literature, such as *Huckleberry Finn* and *Walden,* extols the rebel. "I did it my way," sang Frank Sinatra in a classic popular song.

Authority

It will not come as a surprise that a society that admires independence and progress does not have an automatic respect for authority. What deference people in authority do command is based on their actual powers rather than on their age, wisdom, or dignity. Old people are often seen as behind the times. It's instead the young who are expected to have special insight into the modern world. Not many American adults would consider consulting their parents before making a decision. They are more likely to consult their children!

After all, it was by overthrowing the King of England that the United States was born, and suspicion of authority has remained a pillar of American life. This attitude has helped establish the USA as the birthplace of innovations that have changed the world. If a better way of doing something comes along, we unsentimentally jettison the old way. But we also jettison people. In a society that changes as fast as ours, experience simply does not have the value that it does in traditional societies.

However, independent as Americans like to consider themselves, in the area of work they are not. Most corporations operate in a dictatorial manner and are not expected to accommodate complexities in employees' personal lives. If an executive's responsibilities require sudden travel, family obligations become secondary. Very long work hours are common. Most people think employers have a right to make these demands; the employee after all retains the freedom to find another job.

Land of the Too-Free

"I think one person should end where the other begins," said one immigrant to the United States. Many foreigners agree that American freedom is excessive. Americans tend to leap to the conclusion that any limitation on their rights is an attack on the American way of life. Out on the frontier you could do anything you wanted because nobody was around to notice. (The true frontiersman picked up stakes and moved as soon as he could smell his neighbor's smoke.)

We are a rights-based society (rather than rule-based or group-based). We don't object to following rules, but we want to know that they're fair and the same for everyone. The idea that some people could have privileges that others don't infuriates your average American. Children are taught from a young age to "stick up for your rights."

These equal rights are essential to the idea of America as a nation in which "all men are created equal." You may argue that equal rights are irrelevant in the face of great income disparity (as the French say, "So what if the rich have the same right to sleep under bridges as the poor?"), but we like to think that making money is a right open to all.

In light of all this, one would think that the corporate scandals that led to the bankruptcies of Enron and WorldCom would have led to a furious popular demand for more corporate accountability. In fact, while there was a lot of clucking, there was not – and is not likely to be – much new regulation. Fairness is important, but we don't think it's fair for businesses to be constricted. It has taken a long time to convince the public that free enterprise does not mean a company should be free to pollute the air, foul the rivers, and destroy the forests. Such problems, of course, are not unique to this society.

The right to self-expression is one we take very seriously. An art show that depicts Jesus Christ in an offensive manner may attract few viewers, but there is support for the artist's right to paint and show what she wants. Graffiti is even defended by some people on the grounds that it is a form of self-expression.

The Puritan Tradition

Although we have gone from a rural society to an urban one, many American values remain the traditional ones established by the European settlers in the 17th century.

The Puritans, a stern Christian sect, were among the first and most lasting settlers. Their values were well suited to survival in a strange new world: self-reliance, hard work, frugal living, and the guidance of the individual conscience.

In addition, the Puritans considered earthly success a sign of God's favor and saw no conflict between making money and entering the kingdom of heaven. Americans continue to have few ideas about the holiness of poverty. It's a puritanical idea that people get what they deserve (adding to the difficulties of being poor or handicapped in the USA).

The Puritans would not have smiled on the conspicuous consumption of today, but they would have admired the unrelenting effort that goes into the acquisition of goods. Americans respect businesspeople. An Englishman who has made enough money may well be happy to retire to his country home. The American only wants to go on making more money, driven as much by the Puritan work ethic (often called "the Protestant work ethic") as by the desire for more money.

The Puritan values still referred to today usually refer to a prudishness towards sex and enjoyment. Although the Puritans were not actually against good times, they did feel that people were basically sinful, and spontaneity revealed their inner wickedness. Today, to call someone "Puritanical" is generally not meant as a compliment, as it suggests that he or she is strait-laced and no fun.

However, Americans are positively schizophrenic about sex. Mass culture makes it look as if sex is completely open and free. Yet nothing will bring Child Protective Services to your door faster than the suggestion of inappropriate sexual behavior around children, and charges of sexual harassment in business are taken very seriously. Infidelity in marriage is the rationale for many divorces.

Efficiency: Time Is Money

If there is anything that warms the American heart, it's efficiency. Henry Ford was long regarded as a hero for implementing the assembly line. The assembly line reduced workers to cogs of machinery and ignored their boredom, but it produced goods fast.

"Time is money," we say. Nothing is more American than the supermarket. Food is prepackaged, and shopping is impersonal, but the efficiency of the operation produces lower prices and less shopping time. The food's lack of taste has not created much customer resistance.

Fast-food operations calculate ways of saving a few seconds in each customer's waiting time. It's not just that we're impatient; lunch hours are short, day cares charge extra if parents are late, and if the meter runs out, there's no getting out of paying the ticket.

Even when we're relaxing, we're watching the clock. If I go out to dinner in Spain, I won't expect any food to arrive at my table for an hour, and nobody will be surprised if dinner takes four hours. Here, even at a fancy restaurant, I want to be served promptly and able to leave within two hours. I want to get more things done at home before the night is over.

Time Waits for No Man

According to anthropologist Edward T. Hall, we are a monochronic culture, meaning we operate according to schedules, doing one thing at a time. Sticking to the schedule is more important than the human interruptions to it. When the bell rings, the class is over, no matter how interesting the discussion at that moment.

There are some other Asian countries at least as efficient as the USA, but vast parts of the world cannot conceive of our concept of time. Time is all-important to us. We think of ourselves as people who are going places. Tomorrow is not going to be like today. Tomorrow, we'd like to be way down the road, and speed is going to get us there, not standing around chatting.

Consequently, we have come to see only practical and profitable activity as truly valuable. "How has so Spartan a philosophy descended on an age that hoped to make machines do all the useful work while man enjoyed his leisure?" asked Walter Kerr in his book, *The Decline of Pleasure.*

It does seem that Americans often lack the capacity to enjoy their achievements. We find more satisfaction in acquiring the trappings of the leisure life than in leisure itself. Activity – rather than family or community – gives us our identities, and very few people are able to rest on their laurels. The Puritan values still dominate.

The No-Status Society

In a status society, people learn their places and gain some dignity and security from having a place in the social order. Americans, however, are taught not to recognize their places and to constantly assert themselves. This can manifest itself in positive ways – hard work and innovation – but also in ongoing dissatisfaction. "Democratic institutions most successfully develop sentiments of envy in the human heart," wrote de Tocqueville.

As an American is always striving to change his lot, he never fully identifies with any group. We have no expressions such as in China where "the fat pig gets slaughtered," or in Japan, where "the nail that sticks out gets hammered down." Here, nearly everybody is trying to stick out, which limits closeness between people. We say, "It's the squeaky wheel that gets the grease." According to Alan Roland, author of *In Search of Self in India and Japan,* in the United States "a militant individualism has been combined with enormous social mobility," leaving very little group identity.

"Identity is the number one national problem here," writes Eva Hoffman, the Polish-born author of *Lost in Translation.* "Many of my American friends feel they don't have enough of it. They often feel worthless or they don't know how they feel."

Loneliness is very common. Many people live by themselves and

21

a great many spend nearly every evening alone. Telephones, televisions and computers ease the isolation, and most people have a few friends, but a sense of belonging to a group is largely absent.

However, to someone who feels oppressed in another culture, American life can look wonderful. "Americans have a blank check, on which they can write anything they want," concluded one foreigner after ten years here.

Discontent

If you can never be content with your station, you are never satisfied. The idea of equality is an inspiration, but people can be tricked by it. No success is good enough. Not everybody can reach the top, and those who don't blame themselves.

At best, a status society teaches that every place is worthy; in ours none is. The fear of failure in itself arouses widespread insecurity. Failure in this society is more shameful than poverty in a status society because failure is assumed to be a person's own fault.

The Status Seekers

"I just wanted to find a place where I would be accepted," said an East German who is happily settled in San Francisco. He is delighted that you don't have to be a doctor to be treated with respect and that people don't care who your father is. But the myth of equality should not fool anyone into thinking that America doesn't have a class system. We do, and speech, dress and level of education are strong markers. But it's a very fluid system, and penetration at most levels is possible for nearly anyone with enough money. Equipped with the money, one can acquire the taste, style, and ideas that mark each class and launch a quick ascent of the social ladder.

There do exist a few clubs, societies and debutante balls which require old money for entry. People whose families were among the early arrivals in America may let it be known, but in point of fact, such lineage doesn't mean much (politicians prefer to advertise their humble beginnings), and one's level in society can be – like so many other things in American life – determined by one's own efforts. (Of course, only a few people actually do go from the bottom to the top. Most of the jockeying around is for levels in the middle class.)

One must speak correct English to progress upward socially, but correct English is not nearly as hard to learn as, for instance, correct Japanese. Unlike many other languages, the word "you" is the same no matter whom you are addressing. There are certain accents that will take you further than others, but few leave a person out of the running altogether.

Money is the key to social position, and it is nearly impossible to be upper class without it (with the possible exception of Southern aristocrats). Thus the seriousness of money. If I make a lot of money, I can drive a Mercedes, buy a big house, and join a country club. I will be accepted, not just because I have the money, but because the money proves that I have performed in society at a high level. If I am truly socially ambitious, and have enough money to give large amounts to prestigious charities, I can hire a promoter who will guide me in an assault on high society. If I am hard-working, successful, generous, and amusing on top of it all, nobody will mind how low-class my origins may have been. I would certainly do better not to pretend to advantages I did not have.

However, every generalization has exceptions, and not quite everyone admires money-makers. There are those who subscribe to a different code, called Class X by Paul Fussell in his book *Class*. Usually artists, intellectuals, or eccentrics, members of Class X do their best to disdain the values of the rich. And yet, few are entirely unaffected by money envy.

Conformity

Despite the emphasis on independence, Americans do care a good deal what the world thinks of them. Only through the eyes of others can success have significance. The theory of culture analyst David

Riesman (author of *The Lonely Crowd*) is that Americans are no longer primarily governed by inner values handed down through generations. Instead, he thinks Americans have become outer-directed people – guided not by their own consciences but by the opinions of others. To be liked, or at least envied, is crucial.

The Contradictions

The alert visitor will quickly note much that seems contradictory in American life. Freedom of the press has not produced a well-informed public. We're proud of our democracy, but voter turnout is one of the lowest in any democracy. Despite our wealth, we have people sleeping in the streets. Americans are friendly, but neighbors don't stop to chat. Supplied by the world's richest farmlands, America's cuisine leaves much to be desired.

The social commentator Paul Goodman aptly wrote decades ago, "America has a high standard of living of low average quality." Despite the luxuries and conveniences Americans enjoy, our lives are not elegant. Even the very rich often do their own shopping, cooking, and washing up and may afterwards sit down to watch *Jeopardy* on TV. At the same time, the United States also has plenty of high culture, with operas, ballets, and symphonies equal to any in the world. There is also an extraordinary variety available, as might be expected of a country of immigrants. Whether you're looking for Armenian Folk Dance or a zither society, it will be going on somewhere.

Expect also to find innumerable exceptions to any of my claims about Americans. Just as not every Japanese is hard-working and deferential to superiors, nor every Chinese devoted to family, not every American is ambitious, patriotic, money-grubbing, or even unsophisticated.

— Chapter Two —

AMERICAN ORIGINS

The only real natives in the USA are the American Indians (now often called "Native Americans"). The rest of us spring from families who immigrated to this country within recent history.

Among Caucasians (or Whites), the English were the earliest arrivals, settling the first permanent colony in 1607. They were soon followed by Spanish, Dutch, French, Scottish, Irish, and German settlers. In the 19th century, great numbers of Irish and Chinese immigrated, escaping famines at home. Thereafter, there were waves of Scandinavians, Italians, Russians, Jews, and Greeks. Most of these people arrived poor and stayed poor; the high levels of immigration kept wages minimal. In 1922, Congress set quotas, repealed in 1943, that favored Anglo-Saxons and virtually barred Asians and Africans.

The ancestors of African-Americans (or Blacks) were brought here forcibly from Africa as slaves. Slave-trading was outlawed after 1807 and therefore the families of Black Americans have been here longer than most. The slaves were freed by the Civil War, which ended in 1865.

Statistics show that, legally at least, immigrants from Mexico, India, China, the Phillipines, and Vietnam now predominate, once again changing the ethnic make-up of the country. Illegal immigrants arrive in large numbers from Mexico and Central America, slipping in through the southern border and adding to a large, low-paid labor pool.

Choice Grain

It is an axiom among Americans that we are an exceptional people because our forebears were those with the pluck to abandon their native lands and start anew here. As early as 1668, a William Stoughton wrote that God "sifted a whole nation [England] that he might send choice grain over into this wilderness."

The American humorist H. L. Mencken argued instead that "the majority of non-Anglo-Saxon immigrants since the revolution, like the majority of Anglo-Saxon immigrants before the revolution, have been, not the superior men of their native lands, but the botched and unfit." It was Mencken's view that it was easy to get ahead in America because the competition was third-rate. Unlikely as this is, it is a nice counter-balance to the arrogance Americans sometimes display.

The American sense of superiority can be very annoying to foreigners. Since the collapse of the Soviet Union, the US is now indubitably the world's most powerful nation. For a number of reasons, America is increasingly unpopular in many countries of the world. Fortunately, people often distinguish between the American government, which seems to smaller countries like a bully, and Americans, who are generally well-liked.

When Christopher Columbus, celebrated as the discoverer of America, landed in the West Indies in 1492, he found a generous and friendly people whom he called Indians (because he thought he had discovered the westward route to India). He was not kind to them. He killed some, captured others, and enslaved still more to mine for gold.

When the English settlers arrived in the 17th century, many Indians mistakenly thought there could be room for both themselves and the Europeans; the Indians did not understand the concept of private property that drove the newcomers. They also lacked European firepower, and when driven to defend their land, their bows and arrows proved no match for guns.

Directly and indirectly, the Whites massacred the Indians throughout the first two hundred years of their occupation, until the Indian population was reduced to a small proportion of its original size and pushed onto reservations in the infertile west. The last major battle wasn't fought until 1890, but it was clear much earlier that the Land of the Brave had passed to European hands.

American culture acquired a few agricultural tips and some place names from the Indians, but little else. Our language, institutions, and religion came directly from Europe. For many years so did the livestock, fine clothes and furniture, and literature and music.

The Declaration of Independence

As the victors in a series of wars between European nations, the English became the rulers of northeastern America, but the colonists chafed against English rule and taxation. In 1776, they rebelled. In the famous Declaration of Independence ("We hold these truths to be self-evident, that all men are created equal; that they are endowed by their Creator with certain inalienable rights; that among these, are life, liberty, and the pursuit of happiness"), the colonists declared themselves an independent nation. Five years of fighting ensued – the

War of Independence – at the end of which the British surrendered and went home, and the original thirteen colonies became a free nation, the United States of America.

The United States Constitution

In 1789, the American government was formally established according to the United States Constitution, which includes the Bill of Rights. The Bill upholds individual rights against those of the government. The Constitution is vastly quoted in American life; the most frequently quoted parts are those that deal with freedom of religion, free speech, freedom of assembly, and freedom of the press.

It is because of these constitutional rights that prayer is not allowed in schools; that newspapers may criticize the government; that the police may not search your home without a warrant; and that any group may form a political party. The determination of constitutional rights lies with the Supreme Court, which decides how the Constitution relates to specific cases.

The system of government outlined in the Constitution derived from English traditions – limitation of executive power, bicameral legislature, trial by jury, and protection of individual rights. Although some assert that the system has best served the interests of the landowners who created it, the system has, nevertheless, provided a government of unusual stability.

States' Rights

Many rights and responsibilities were reserved for individual states, which causes confusion for visiting foreigners. Many laws (such as the laws regarding divorce, drinking, wages, guns, education, and driving) vary from state to state. When corporations establish their headquarters in a particular state, they must follow the laws of that state. Each state has its own school and taxation system.

One Creed/One Nation

The ideals of democracy, equality, and freedom served an important purpose as the country grew older. As a nation, America was singularly bereft of unifying concepts. Whereas most peoples are unified by race, language, culture, traditions, and history, America's immigrant population had little in common other than the initiative to get ahead. In the days when communication was slow, the country was too big for a centralized government. Instead, democracy became the faith, the unifying theme, of the new nation. America may be the only country in the world founded on a creed.

During the first half of the 19th century, the doctrine of equal rights was developed to mythical proportions. A. A. Bennet wrote in 1827, "We may look forward to the period when the spark kindled in America shall spread and spread, till the whole earth be illuminated by its light." Individual liberty, in the American mind, became synonymous with America, and Americans consider themselves the world's freest people.

Until recently, Americans were generally very proud of their democratic political system. We thought of our government as uniquely democratic, run by representatives of the people, chosen in honest elections. This was not necessarily so, but it was not much called into question.

Today, the amount of campaign money required to win high office is so great that candidates are forced to seek money from those who have it. Without money, a candidate or national office can't buy television advertisements, and those who don't advertise on TV make little impression on voters. Consequently, there is widespread opinion that corporations and the very rich acquire disproportionate power through making campaign contributions. It is believed that businesses with special interests in the laws that are passed get the ear of their legislators through these donations.

Some states limit contribution amounts, and a new law was passed in Washington in 2002 limiting corporate contributions. However,

29

there are loopholes in the new law, and nobody expects that money will not continue to affect politics. One particular factor has been the Supreme Court's ruling that the right of free speech gives people the right to spend as much of their own money as they want to win office.

While anyone over the age of 18 is eligible to vote, fewer than half the voters usually do. Those who do not vote sometimes claim that neither one of the major parties, Democrats or Republicans, serves their interests. Yet no notable third party has emerged. Because we have a winner-take-all system, offices only go to those who have won a majority of the votes, unlike in a parliamentary system.

Although the Democrats look for support among working people, labor unions, and ethnic minorities, and the Republicans get many of their votes from white Southerners, the religious Right, and corporate boardrooms, the two parties are, in fact, not much different. Both regularly promise lower taxes, a strong military, free trade, and smaller government. Since September 11, 2001, however, the government has taken a strong role in national domestic security and has assumed new powers in the course of fighting the War on Terrorism.

Foreigners often find Americans naive about politics and ignorant of foreign affairs. Do not expect that Americans will know anything about your country's government, wherever it is.

But Some Weren't So Equal

In reality, constitutional rights have been unevenly distributed throughout our history. Each immigrant group has been subjected to discrimination; the Chinese in particular suffered from laws that once prohibited Chinese land ownership, marriage with whites, and other such rights. African-Americans have had a long and unique history of discrimination. Women were not allowed to vote until 1920, and it is only in the last twenty-five years that discriminatory laws against women have been struck down. Today, all discrimination according to race, color, sex, or creed is illegal, but it nonetheless continues in various forms.

Intractable as America's race problem seems, at least philosophically we are against prejudice. Most Americans do not accept the idea that some people are born inferior to others, and it is not socially acceptable to make slighting statements about people on the basis of their race. (However, people are not as delicate about references to nationality, and jokes about the Polish, the Irish, the Chinese, the Scottish, etc., are widespread.) To dislike people because of their color is considered ignorant and stupid, and no responsible public speaker makes outright racist statements.

Most foreigners interviewed for this book (from all parts of the world) held that racism has not been a big problem for them. Today there are many more women, African-Americans, Hispanics, and other ethnic groups in government than in years past; it's the economic pie that has not been so readily shared.

Black Americans

The lot of African-Americans has been the most difficult of any American group. Until the Civil War, they lived under one of the most brutalizing versions of slavery in history. Afterwards, they began their lives as free people without property, skills, education, or civil rights, in a land in which they were widely regarded as inferior.

In the Old South (the Southeast) especially, where most of them lived, blacks were segregated. They were not allowed to eat in white restaurants, stay in white hotels, or use white bathrooms. Schools, parks, and swimming pools were all segregated. The worst jobs were reserved for blacks. It was not until 1955 when a tired black woman, Rosa Parks, refused to give up a seat on the bus to a white man that the civil rights movement started to gain any ground in integrating public facilities. In 1964, an omnibus Civil Rights Bill was passed by Congress, banning public segregation.

African-Americans also fought a long struggle in the North against unofficial segregation, which was not so blatant as in the South, but has proven perhaps even more persistent. They lived in separate neighborhoods and were the last hired and first fired. Attempts to guarantee African-Americans places in public universities and workplaces, called "affirmative action", have been stalled recently and outlawed in some places, on the grounds that in no way should race be a factor in assessing potential candidates.

Homosexuals

Homosexuals were disdained in America for many years and only recently has public opinion changed. Thanks largely to a civil rights movement similar to that of African-Americans and women, the law has recognised that to discriminate against someone because of "sexual preference" is as bad as discriminating on the basis of color.

Many gays and lesbians, however, still feel that prejudice requires them to conceal their homosexuality. Nonetheless, the progress towards equal rights in the past thirty years has been tremendous, and there are now openly gay and lesbian people in police departments and even in the US Congress. Gays have particularly won admiration by their fortitude and activism in the face of the AIDS crisis. It is notable how many of the men who died of AIDS have, even at a young age, been prominent in their fields.

The Rise of the USA

The United States, despite its burgeoning wealth, was not of importance to the world at large until the twentieth century. Foreigners often considered Americans ignorant, uncultured, and unsophisticated. Before modern communication systems, Americans were too far from the European capitals to follow their fashions and too busy working the land to care about them.

After the two world wars in the 20th century, however, the USA could no longer be regarded as a backwater. Whatever its cultural deficits, its farms provided food for the world, and its factories exported much of the world's manufactured goods. American jazz and American movies stamped the USA onto world consciousness.

The Vietnam War

The Vietnam War, which engaged American troops from 1964 to 1973, caused much conflict between Americans. It gave rise to the largest anti-war movement the country had ever known; there was acute division in the country between those who did and did not support the war. At the end, despite the deaths of 50,000 Americans and the dropping of seven million tons of bombs, America withdrew in defeat. There is still bitterness in the country over the war, particularly on the part of Vietnam veterans, who feel betrayed both by the government that sent them to war and by the populace which treated them with contempt when they came home.

The Sixties

The Vietnam War gave rise to a rebellious generation. Students led the anti-war movement and from questioning the government's Vietnam policy went on to question the entire history of the United States as it had been represented in their history books. The civil rights movement had been a precursor of the anti-war movement, and the anti-war movement, in turn, led to support of women's rights, Indian rights, and farm workers' rights, among others.

A broad spectrum of young people – who became known as "hippies" experimented with communal living, sexual freedom and drugs, while proclaiming the power of love. Long hair and imaginative clothes distinguished hippies from "straights." Rock music provided the theme songs.

However, the establishment hardly stumbled, and by the late 1970s the aging young rebels found it politic to join society as it was. Society had certainly changed – for economic as well as political reasons. The affluence of the 1960s was over. Many more women held jobs than ever before. In some respects the appearance of egalitarianism was more pronounced. Many social rituals were out, dress was more casual, and discrimination less blatant. But the inequities of wealth and privilege remained; some of the Sixties' generation went on to fight for environmental causes, while others turned inward to focus on personal self-fulfilment.

End of an Era?

For over a hundred years, the USA enjoyed extraordinary economic growth, and we came to expect this growth would continue forever. We got used to having an ever-increasing Gross National Product to solve our problems. We could talk about equality without having to make sacrifices.

Taxes remained low, individuals profited, and there was enough left over to pay for social programs. But after 1972, there was a serious recession, combined with double-digit inflation. It wasn't until the 1990s that the country really recovered, and the recovery didn't last long. Fast on the heels of extraordinary stock market highs, the USA followed Asia into a recession at the start of the 21st century.

Social services in the USA have never been on the same level as Europe's, and the safety net for the system's losers is inadequate. In the 1990s social services were cut back even further, in the name of making big government smaller. Union membership is minimal, and few people have job security. As welfare benefits are much more limited now than they used to be, unemployment quickly leads to an upsurge in homelessness.

September 11, 2001

On September 11, 2001, Muslim extremists hijacked four US airliners. Two planes were deliberately crashed into New York's World Trade Center, which both collapsed, and another plane plunged into the Pentagon in Washington, America's military headquarters. Passengers of the fourth plane overpowered their hijackers, and the plane crashed in a Pennsylvania field. The combined death toll from the terrorist attacks exceeded 3,000.

The effect on the USA was devastating. Americans had never before been attacked on their own soil in such a manner. It became clear that Osama Bin Laden, the exiled Saudi Arabian leader of the terrorist organization Al-Qaeda, was behind the attacks. The US turned the full force of its military against Osama Bin Laden and his Afghanistan hosts, the Taliban, a month after the September 11 attacks.

The Taliban was easily defeated, but at this writing Al-Qaeda remains operative, along with other terrorist organizations. Americans are now aware of how frighteningly vulnerable they are to terrorist attacks. Our open society has made it surprisingly easy for foreigners to come, open bank accounts, take flying lessons, and hijack planes. The War on Terrorism extends to countries suspected of harboring terrorists, but nobody really knows how to stop them.

In fact, the mentality of terrorists is incomprehensible to us. President George W. Bush said it's the "face of evil attacking liberty," and that seems to be explanation enough for many people. But there are others who wonder how much US foreign policy contributes to the problem, whether disparities between rich and poor breeds religious extremism, and whether the basic conflict is essentially religious or whether we are facing clashing civilizations.

There are fears both in and outside the US Congress that important American freedoms may be compromised in the effort to track down terrorists. While we do not want our enemies freely plotting deadly attacks by e-mail, neither do we want the government reading everybody's e-mail.

Chapter Three

VARIETIES OF AMERICAN LIFE

People have asked me, "how can you generalize about America when there are so many regional differences?" Americans tend to see most American customs as normal human behavior and the few elements that vary as the cultural part. In fact, the similarities in customs across the land, big as it is, are vastly greater than the differences.

It is the culture of the white middle class that is reflected in this book because it is their values and practices that shape America. Although many of our citizens are neither white nor middle class, most nonetheless subscribe to the majority outlook. Even people born elsewhere begin to change their ways after a few years' exposure. "I knew I was becoming an American," says an Iranian, "when I started wanting to have time to myself."

Regional Differences

Regional differences, such as they are, are most notable in the South. Family counts for more there, and money less. Time is a little slower, hospitality a bit fuller, the work ethic slightly less full-blown. The South lost a war that the North won (the Civil War or War Between the States), which has given the white Southerner a heritage of failure and defeat that Northerners are exempt from.

Yet the South does not feel like a foreign place. Airports are identical, pay phones operate as expected, and department stores display the same labels. The same hotel and fast food chains thrive all over the country. In the commercial centers, where international businessmen gather, only the hot weather may indicate it's the South. Anyone looking for regional variety should abandon the cities and explore small towns. Throughout the USA, and especially in the South, there are rural communities where the values described in this book appear subordinate to family ties and tradition.

Southerners were once considered to be more racist than Northerners, but this is no longer necessarily the case. Not only have attitudes changed in the South, the diversity is fast increasing. It was once hard to find a decent egg roll below the Mason-Dixon line, but the number of Asians has grown geometrically in recent years, particularly in pockets in and around large cities, creating a much more diverse culinary scene. Visitors are likely to enjoy the famous Southern warmth and politeness. However, warns a disaffected Southerner, "Don't believe everything they say."

Southerners tend to be effusive and friendly. However, they are less direct and frank than Northerners, less apt to tell you about their neuroses, and their family problems. They are more apt to have deep roots in the places where they live and to have an extended family living nearby. Consequently, social circles may be closed to newcomers – foreigners and American-born as well. Life in the South can prove lonely for those without secure contacts.

New Englanders or Yankees (in the Northeast) are conventionally

37

the opposite of Southerners. They are supposedly reserved and quiet, more apt to speak in monosyllables than to babble. They are traditionalists, preferring the old to the new. They make no promises they cannot keep. They are slow to accept newcomers but will in time, should the newcomers prove reliable. The foreigner living in New England needs only patience. Friendships once developed are lasting.

New Yorkers (residents of New York City) are in a category of their own, with a reputation for being impatient, fast-talking, and rude. Nowhere else in the country is it necessary to put one's head down and elbows out to jam onto a subway or bus. Money talks particularly loudly in New York. Do not waste your time being offended by the rudeness of New Yorkers. Try, instead, to appreciate their wit, which New Yorkers have in abundance. Like many cities, New York can be a lonely place, so friends become very close as a result.

Midwesterners are credited with being plain-speaking, casual, and conservative. One thinks of Midwesterners as unglamourous but genuine. Midwesterners don't like "phonies" so in the Midwest we can all relax and be ourselves.

Californians, on the contrary, are expected to be trendy, superficial, and empty-headed. The beautiful blondes and the Hollywood money are concentrated in the southern part of the state. Californians pride themselves on open-mindedness and as the state is home to a vast mix of peoples, you should find ready acceptance wherever you're from.

Whatever grains of truth there might be in these stereotypes, you may have to work pretty hard to observe any of these differences. New England is full of chatty, emotional people and the South has its share of cold and quiet ones. Americans are just too mobile for regional differences to live up to their reputations.

Accents

The most notable difference among the regions is the accent. Northerners make fun of the slow Southern speech with its drawn-out vowels, and Southerners think the fast, clipped speech of Northerners sounds rude. A Western accent is an amalgam of many and not easily placed. Then there are numerous localized accents – those from Maine, Boston, and Brooklyn are all distinctive. Yet the vocabularies vary little, and few of these accents are difficult to understand for anyone who speaks fluent English. A large number of the people in every region speak without a trace of the local accent.

Food

Food, too, has a few local distinctions. You must go to the South to find hominy grits (a form of corn). New York City, heavily under the influence of the Jewish deli, serves up a vast number of hot pastrami (smoked and seasoned beef) sandwiches. You won't get many crawfish outside of Louisiana. But 90% of the dishes on any menu in the country are the same everywhere. Freezing, storage, and growing techniques have seen to it that if Americans like something, they can have it wherever they go.

Ethnic Groups

Cultural differences between ethnic groups are probably greater than regional differences. Many African-Americans have retained a somewhat separate culture with distinctive language and strong ties to the extended family. Several French writers have noted that the conversational style of African-Americans, with its lively repartee, is closer to the French manner than the more plodding delivery of the white American.

Native American tribes pride themselves on having rejected the grasping ways of the European settlers. Some, living on reservations, continue to speak their own language, practice their own religion and ceremonies, and follow customs extremely foreign to those of white Americans. That they have continued to do so despite several centuries' efforts of missonaries and government first to annihilate and then to assimilate them, is a testament to the strength of their cultures.

39

Scattered about in obscure pockets of land, most notably in the South, are traditional white communities where a great deal of what is said in this book would not apply. Here and there, religious groups live communally in defiance of the American passion for private property. Unless you are an anthropologist, you are unlikely to meet any of these groups.

Less obscure are large urban communities of Chinese, Japanese, Irish, Poles, Russians, Vietnamese, Italians, Mexicans, etc. In towns and cities you can also find enclaves of Scandinavians, Hungarians, Germans, Laotians and scores of other nationalities. Each group, to a certain extent, manages to retain aspects of their native cuisines, holidays, and habits.

Despite its size, the USA is not as diverse a country as we sometimes like to think. We have institutions and businesses that impose unity on us all. People who have grown up in this country have gone to the same schools, watched the same television shows and movies, read the same magazines, shared the same historical events, taken in the same nightly news, worked for the same companies, been subjected to the same advertisements and celebrated the same holidays, in addition to speaking the same language.

Americanization

In many ways, American habits are a product of affluence and are spreading to other parts of the world. Extended families are less likely to live together when they can afford separate homes. It doesn't seem so bad to be alone when you're home with cable television, an internet connection, a portable telephone, and plenty to read. Small families indulge their children more than large ones ever could, and children who own cars become less dependent on their parents.

In other countries, when jobs become available for young people in distant cities, when television begins to dominate home life, when ready-made foods appear in the markets, the culture appears more "American" – although the resemblance could be entirely superficial.

Chapter Four

HOW TO TELL AN AMERICAN

How is it that on any train platform in the world everyone can pick out the Americans? Despite our different heritage, there is a style that marks us. We have shy people and bold, talkative and taciturn, and yet the quality of "Americanness" is unmistakable. The expression, the gestures, and the posture all give us away even before we speak.

Says one Britwho has lived around the world, "Americans have an enthusiastic look. They feel empowered, and the looks on their faces say, 'I can make a difference.' Nobody else has that special kind of confidence."

The Famous Friendliness

One distinguishing characteristic of Americans is our openness to strangers. Practically everyone agrees that Americans are friendly. Very few Americans care to put on snobbish airs, even if they secretly regard themselves as being far above the crowd. Part of being superior is to appear not to think you are. The president of the USA emphasizes what a regular guy he is. A college professor who goes fishing with plumbers will brag about it; he too is one of the boys, not an intellectual in an ivory tower.

Friendly – Not Friends

Saying hello doesn't commit you to anything. It only asserts that you subscribe to our code of democracy. Friendliness should not be confused with friendship. Many foreigners slip up here, and mistakenly think that all that warmth means they're going to have lots of friends. Then they become disillusioned and decide we're terribly superficial and shallow in our friendships. But most of the people we refer to as "friends" are really acquaintances. True friends are not easier to come by here than anywhere else.

Emotions

Americans do not see the need to hide their emotions. On the contrary, they often seem to be exaggerating them. Enthusiasm, for instance, rises to levels of seeming unbelievability ("It's great to see you, you look fabulous, let's have lunch soon.") These glad sentiments don't mean much more than, "It is agreeable to be having this exchange on the street corner, and I may or may not be serious about lunch."

Happiness here can be loudly proclaimed in big smiles, gestures and statements: "This is marvellous, best news I've ever heard." Unlike many Asians, Americans smile only around good news or happy feelings. An American smiles often, but not when embarrassed or confused, nor would an American deliver bad news with a smile. Bad news comes with a somber, concerned expression.

Expressing sadness does not come as easily to us. Sorrow interferes with our upbeat, optimistic view of life, and people who are sad do not find ready acceptance. Friends may try to cheer a sad person up, but can become quickly frustrated if the sad person doesn't respond.

Touching

Americans are what is known as a "non-contact people." Outside of hugs given in greeting and parting, touching, among adults, is generally limited to occasions when its sexual connotations are acceptable. If in a moment of warmth, a Russian man rests his hand on an American man's thigh, the American is stricken. Could this be an untoward advance? Likewise, two American men would never hold hands. Nor would two American women, although they would not be as put off by the whole idea as men would be.

Latin Americans find us cold in this regard; many Americans are envious of people who can reach out freely and affectionately, but our strong sense of private space inhibits us. In conversation, Americans usually stand at least an arm's length apart and are made uncomfortable by people who press closer (unless the relationship is an intimate one). We are careful not to breathe into people's faces.

Children and pets are caressed freely, but America is currently in the middle of a huge frenzy about child sexual abuse, so one must be careful that nothing appears abnormal about one's affection towards children. Teachers must be particularly careful that nobody suspects a sexual interest in children on the teacher's part. And if there is evidence of parents sexually molesting their children, Child Protective Services may remove those children and jail the offending parent.

Talking

Because it is important to be assertive, Americans speak fairly loudly, at least compared to Thais or Malaysians, for example. Foreigners sometimes mistake the loudness for anger when an American is only trying to make himself understood.

Men slap each other on the back, or squeeze another's shoulder, but they avoid any touching that could appear to have sexual connotations.

Anger itself, within limits, is also more acceptable among Americans than in most cultures. If someone thinks he has been wronged, he may feel called upon to show his feelings. This is not to say that we admire people who are out of control – a temper tantrum is not a pretty sight – but a justifiably angry person will not be condemned whereas someone who "lets people walk all over him" may well be. Some nice guys go far, but you can also become company president despite a reputation for "blowing your top"!

We are taught to look into people's eyes during conversation. Someone who instead looks around or down appears shifty to us, although in actual fact one doesn't stare continuously at the other person but glances elsewhere every few seconds.

Etiquette

As a low-context culture, we don't have many set routines for particular situations. Formality seems undemocratic to us, and Americans dislike rituals of etiquette that recognize class differences. Our easy manners contribute to the fluidity of our society.

Informal, of course, does not mean "mannerless." We would not be any sort of culture if we did not have some agreement as to what nice behavior is. You should refrain from making religious, ethnic, or racial slurs. Don't ignore women or children. Treat people equally. But on the whole, Americans will be very forgiving of awkward manners. We do not have the religious prohibitions that make

Photo: Kristy MacDonald

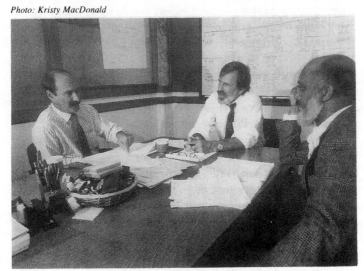

The man on the left may appear angry, but the other two aren't upset by his behavior. They know he is just making a point.

innocent foreign behavior so shocking in some countries. Nothing but the flag is sacred in our public life and even the right to desecrate it is protected.

Politeness

Visitors usually find most Americans, for all their informality, very polite. This reputation seems to rest largely on the great number of "Pleases" and "Thank yous" we deliver, but also on the general recognition given to strangers. One should be considerate of waiters, garage attendants, and household help as well as of doctors and senators. Americans are often shocked to see the peremptory manner in which servants are treated in other countries.

"The way you Americans say 'Thank you' and 'You're welcome' all the time is hypocritical," objected one Chinese man. "You don't really mean it." It's true that we don't mean much by it, but it's an acknowledgement that we don't expect people to do things for us. Even when a service is not optional – such as when receiving change in a store – a person who doesn't give thanks appears rude to an American .

"You're welcome" troubles some newcomers with its suggestion that one has actually done something worthy of thanks. You can always say, "Oh, it was nothing," but if it really was nothing, it's best to stick with "You're welcome."

Of course, whether you consider Americans polite depends on where you come from. Some Japanese find Americans so rude that they think they are being discriminated against when Americans are only acting normally. Politeness also depends on where you are. New Yorkers have a far-reaching reputation for rudeness, although they can also be surprisingly helpful.

Out in public, manners vary a great deal. A lot of attention has been given lately to a rising lack of public civility, particularly among drivers. And foreigners are often appalled at the behavior of children, who commonly are disruptive in public and feel free to speak to their parents in a manner unheard of in many cultures. Surprisingly though, many of these same children grow up to behave quite decently.

Extremes

Americans are not traditionalists, and new ideas can spread like wildfire. Since the 1960s, each generation has felt the need to re-examine the rules of daily behavior and swing away from the way their parents did things. Forty years ago, people believed that children should be seen and not heard, and when seen, should show respect. Then the gospel spread that children who got to express their feelings freely and do what they wanted would grow up to be loving, happy, and creative. This proved not to be necessarily true, and today, numerous books propose limits for children as if it were a brand-new idea.

Communities and extended families don't have much influence, so people who haven't learned a code of behavior at home or school are likely to emerge into adulthood feeling socially awkward. The pendulum is swinging again now, and we are looking favorably at the idea of public civility and predictable rules of etiquette. Thus, with amazement, we now witness etiquette classes for adults as well as children. Ballroom dancing, with its precise steps, is greatly in vogue.

A newspaper column, "Miss Manners," is widely syndicated. We probably will not see gentlemen go back to tipping their hats to the ladies or children leaping to their feet when their elders enter a room, but good manners are appreciated. You may be assured that your own gracious manners will be found delightful.

Taboos

There are few taboos for newcomers to think about. Nobody has to worry about using the left hand, showing the soles of the feet, touching someone's head, or any of those prohibitions that seem so mysterious to Americans abroad. There are, however, a few socially unacceptable types of behavior.

- Do not belch, that is, let gas upward out of the stomach while making an attention-catching noise. Flatulence should be as discreet as humanly possible.
- Do not spit. You may well see someone spit in the street, but you will know from the act that this person has no class. A gentleman does not spit, even in his own backyard.
- Do not make noise chewing gum. This is lowly behavior, widely indulged in, but objectionable nonetheless. Chewing gum in itself is not charming.
- Do not stare (gaze fixedly at someone you are not talking to).
- Do cover your mouth when you cough, sneeze, or yawn.
- Do not whistle at women.
- Properly, gentlemen should take off their hats indoors.

The Casual Life

Informality pervades our culture. The forms of our language do not change when we address a superior, as they do in many languages. People dress casually as much as possible. We use slang in nearly all circumstances. We slouch in chairs, lean against walls, and put our feet on desks.

There are, however, boundaries. In church, you sit up straight. You do not use slang before a judge. If your boss comes into your office and puts his feet up on your desk, you are flattered; he regards you as an equal. But you don't put your feet up on his desk. A lot of these distinctions are subtle, and foreigners can step on toes by trying to become American-casual before understanding the culture well.

Our degrees of casualness do leave a lot of room for confusion. Teachers who are informal ("Call me Janet") and friendly and open with their students want to be liked; they do not wish to be treated as any other friend. Should students respond by becoming too personal or forward with their teacher, they may discover a frosty barrier.

Boye de Mente in his insightful book, *Etiquette and Ethics in Japan,* depicts the Japanese as difficult to penetrate on the outside and

Photo: Kristy MacDonald

Sneezing, coughing, and yawning all require that the mouth be covered. The hand may be open or in a fist. It is nice to also say, "Excuse me."

very open on the inside. Americans, he says, are the opposite. The top layer is very open and anyone can penetrate it. It is the inner layers that are hard to crack. Some Americans remain forever impenetrable.

Relaxed? No

Most of my countrymen will be eager to assure you that they live in a very casual, relaxed manner. This may be far from true. They may keep their houses spotlessly clean, never open their doors to strangers, and live a rigidly planned life, but it remains an article of faith that the good life is the relaxed one. Relaxing is a synonym for having a good

49

time, as seen in the many advertisements which picture people lying around in the sun. However, much as people look forward to relaxing, they rarely actually do it.

It's hard to take it easy when time represents opportunity. The conviction that you succeed or fail by your own efforts – rather than by the whims of fate – is one that adds a high degree of tension to life. And without family and community to fall back on, success of some sort becomes critical.

The whole concept of achievement, whether in career or hobby (e.g. gourmet cooking), makes passing the hours in idle conversation seem like a waste of time. As that sage Ben Franklin said, "Time lost is never found again." Too much sitting around, and the American gets nervous and wants to be up doing something. Even on vacation, Americans want to "improve each shining hour." Said an Indian married to an American, "We went to see the Grand Canyon and as soon as we got there my wife wanted to go rushing down to the bottom. These Americans never relax."

A Tanzanian living in the USA says, "I have my beeper on 24 hours a day. Even when I'm in bed with my wife, I have to respond within three minutes should it sound. How can I relax?" A group of Italian journalists working in the United States reported that they all followed the same pattern on arriving in the States. At first they were terribly exhilarated by the pace of life. After six months, they were exhausted. How, they wanted to know, do Americans keep up this relentless activity?

It's not just that we work hard. Our leisure activities are equally demanding. Besides the pursuit of health and fitness, any number of adult Americans are taking night classes, attending lectures, involving themselves in children's schools, leading scout troops, running church groups, birdwatching, and redecorating. Weekends are full of camping, sports, and home improvement. Then when we get "all stressed out," we take another course – yoga, meditation, or stress management.

In most cultures, people spend the largest amount of their leisure time sitting around with friends and family, visiting and being visited. We do not. We might like the idea, but we don't have the time.

The person who never relaxes may end up turning to drugs for help, which may be one reason that alcohol, cocaine, marijuana, and other illegal substances are such problems. Television (known as the "boob tube") is another escape and induces a drug-like lethargy almost as effectively as the real drugs.

The family hot tub is a useful antidote to stress. Adapted from Japanese baths, it is a tub full of circulating hot water, in which four or five people can sit. The effectiveness of the hot water is such that nearly anyone can relax in one. (The question on most people's minds when invited to an evening in someone's hot tub is whether or not they will be expected to wear bathing suits. Probably yes. However, if your hosts are nude, you can take your choice as to whether to wear your suit or not. Naturally, you do not stare under any circumstances.)

The Well-Planned Life

Being casual also has nothing to do with leaving matters to chance. The Latin American attitude of "Que sera sera" (What will be will be) is no defense here. We feel the prizes are awarded to the go-getters, the energetic, the forethinking. So many people plan their whole lives with care – career, children, retirement.

The little things are planned too, which is why foreigners can find it so difficult to make social engagements with Americans. Datebooks are full, and the plans for self-improvement often take precedence over the social ones.

Self-Improvement

It is doubtful whether there is another place in the world where people are so intent on improving themselves. Americans' nearly unique belief in progress includes the proposition that individuals can change their natures – or at the very least, their bodies. Our Constitution

51

Gardening is a popular way to make leisure time productive. Besides providing an excuse for being outdoors, the results are highly visible.

guarantees us "life, liberty, and the pursuit of happiness." Not to be happy is not just a misfortune; it is a failure. We want inner peace and contentment, and duty to family is not a good excuse for unhappiness. We believe you should renounce the family if necessary in order to strive for individual fulfillment.

Psychologists say we must love ourselves before we can love other people. So we are trying to.

Foreigners usually think that Americans are quite good at loving themselves already, but they may mistake the outer bluster for the real thing. Actually, the competitive atmosphere in which we live makes people very critical of themselves. Depression is a major problem. Furthermore, the belief in progress suggests that life ought to be constantly getting better and better. As it usually isn't, we must find what's wrong and repair it.

Modes of Repair

Popular psychology has lined the bookshelves with volumes promising to bring happiness into individual lives. Most of them have to do with modes of right thinking. They teach how to be more assertive and to get the things out of life one deserves. Rather incredibly to the foreigners who feel that we're already the most selfish people in the world, many of these 'philosophies' train people how to say "no" when other people make demands on them. A few popular favorites are: *Self Matters* (by the ubiquitous Dr. Phil); *Codependent No More, Boundaries* and *Stand Up For Your Life*.

A perennial favorite for the past 65 years has been *How to Win Friends and Influence People* by Dale Carnegie. It's the basic text book for popularity, and Dale Carnegie courses, which teach the techniques, are flourishing.

Weekend workshops cover all the same subjects that the books do, at much greater cost but promising a nearly instant new self. The past decades saw an emphasis on books and courses that straightforwardly promised to make a person rich. There is instruction in time management, negotiation, sex, and many words have been written on making relationships work and on raising children.

Therapists

When troubles get too big, many Americans go off to see a therapist. There's a broad selection of them: doctors trained in psychoanalysis, psychologists, people with master's degrees in family therapy and in social work. The range of methods used is likewise broad, and the necessary credentials to practice vary by state.

Usually a person visits their therapist once a week for fifty minutes, and the course of therapy can last between a few weeks and a decade, depending on the method and the goals. At best, therapy helps people overcome depression, anxiety, phobias, substance-abuse problems, and to deal successfully with work, family, and relationship issues. At the least, one can expect a therapist to listen intently and give you a sense of being understood. The price is high – $80 an hour and up – although many therapists and clinics will adjust the rate according to income.

Americans do not consider it shameful to go see "a shrink" (short for "headshrinker"). It's a quintessentially American way of dealing with problems. Foreigners are often aghast and say "Why don't they talk to their families or their friends?", but therapists are trained to look at the big picture and find the mysteries behind people's irrational behavior; this in itself is an intriguing undertaking. If you do decide to go in for therapy, be particular about who you choose. Some therapists are much more effective than others.

Prozac and Ritalin

In the last twenty years, antidepressants have been replacing therapy for many. Medical plans appreciate that they're cheaper than therapy. These drugs, of which Prozac is the best known, have become the subject of much debate. Should we really be covering over our social problems by prescribing drugs to a large proportion of the population? Some of the Prozac-takers aren't even particularly depressed but find that the drug enables them to be more successful in life.

Prozac is also prescribed for children and even dogs. And children who are having trouble in school are frequently diagnosed with ADD (Attention Deficit Disorder) for which they are given Ritalin. Ritalin helps them quiet down and concentrate, but many wonder if drugging children is the best solution to a problem with broader implications.

Exercise

A lot of people have concluded that exercise works even better than therapy. It doesn't seem surprising that after several generations of riding around in cars and watching television hour after hour, Americans would discover that they have lost a sense of physical wellbeing.

Some years ago, doctors delivered the news that the post-industrial age had produced physically well cared for but sadly unfit beings. Furthermore, they said, the American heart was in as bad shape as the rest of the muscles. The American male, it seemed, was inclined to drop dead before men in the rest of the Westernized world.

One of the answers, we were told, was aerobic exercise. (Aerobic exercise is the kind that raises the pulse to a certain level for a certain period of time, thus giving the heart itself a workout. It is also said to increase the brain's production of norepinephrines – natural tranquilliszers.) Jogging was the first great craze. Then came stationary bicycles, rowing machines, the stairmaster, and roller blades. Swimming has always been in style. Aerobic dance, in which a roomful of sweating men and women run and kick and jump to loud, throbbing music, has many followers. "Pilates" is a new kind of workout that many swear by.

Health clubs, usually equipped with workout machines, swimming pools and saunas, can be found almost everywhere. Read the agreement carefully if you're thinking of joining one. Many use high-pressure tactics to sign newcomers up for extended periods. Some have initiation fees, large or small. Nearly all have some scheme whereby you can try out the club before joining.

Dieting

Mother Nature, in protecting humans from famine, made fattening foods appealing, and American industry has made fattening foods quick and cheap. People from many cultures get fat here, including ones that have little obesity back in their homelands. According to the Surgeon General, 61% of America's adults and 14% of the children are overweight .

Yet it is fashionable to be very thin. (Whatever you do, don't tell people they look fat.) The effort to be thin while constantly tempted by fattening foods has put many people (usually women) on recurrent

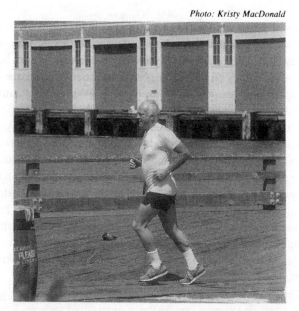

Photo: Kristy MacDonald

Joggers can be seen on city streets from early morning until late at night.

cycles of weight loss and regain.

Despite evidence that at least 95% of the weight lost in dieting is regained, Americans remain irresistibly attracted to new diets and weight-loss gimmicks. The top selling books in this country are cookbooks and diet books.

There is an unfortunate prejudice against fat people, which comes from the viewpoint that the fat person is a person lacking in self-control, rather than the victim of a metabolic problem. Foreigners in particular, surprised to see so much obesity, often suffer from this prejudice.

The Youth Cult

The elderly are also the victims of prejudice. The bias towards youth is so prevalent that even young men with a few grey hairs may dye their hair. At the very top, in the executive boardrooms, signs of age are permissible, but in most endeavors, older people – experience notwithstanding – are at a disadvantage.

Distressing as this is, it is not surprising in a country primarily interested in the new. Old people, who represent continuity with the past, have less to offer here than in a culture where tradition is valued. Young people are not attached to the old ways of doing things, and their flexibility is considered an important asset. In new industries, such as Internet Technology, some of the young people actually do have more experience than their elders.

We have enormous faith in new ideas, new techniques, and new gadgets. If schools aren't trying to solve their problems by imposing new teaching methods, they're trying to solve them by bringing in computers and internet access. Advertisements will make their entire claim for a product the fact that it is new. They don't even have to add "better." To us, "new" assumes "better." If nothing else, young people are newer, and even their unoriginal ideas may look "new".

I have a friend, a very successful editor, who says that because she has reached the age of 40 without becoming an editor-in-chief, she can now reach the top only under the most extraordinary circumstances. Publishers are looking for 35-year-olds to run their shows. Discouraging as this seems, it is, thankfully, not true of every business.

Forever Young

The desperation to look young intensifies yearly. Facelifts, once the province of the very rich, are now undergone by ordinary middle class people. A range of operations tackle other signs of aging.

Wrinkles are the great enemy, and for their elimination millions of dollars of dubious creams and potions are sold. Hair dye has made grey-haired women scarce.

Although most older women wouldn't wear knee socks and miniskirts, they are not expected to adopt age-appropriate garb. No

57

one would think that bright colors were more suitable for a young woman, or that the woman of years should not be wearing tight blue jeans and a blouse with a plunging neckline.

All people like to hear about how very young they look. One views old age as a stage of life when one is not in demand, when one has nothing to contribute. In a society where achievement is everything, those who are past contributing fall from grace.

Good Works

Not all Americans are concentrating on staying young, losing weight and improving themselves. America is also a country in which individuals give a total of more than $109 billion a year to charity, and many give of their time as well. Small, local governments depend largely on unpaid citizens to run them. Public schools, water systems, hospitals, and many other public services are watched over by unpaid boards. Any number of charities – from soup kitchens to drop-in medical clinics – rely on volunteers. And many churches involve their parishioners in a range of good works, which can be anything from tutoring children to delivering a water system to a poor, small town in Guatemala.

This kind of active civic life is very important in a democracy and has been traditional in the US since the colonial days. The people involved generally find it highly rewarding and a source of strong community ties. In fact, there is an argument that America's economic success is built on these social networks.

Unfortunately, civic involvement in the US has fallen by practically every measure – from voting to bowling – since the 1960s. There are some obvious reasons: longer working hours, women in the workforce, long commutes, TV, videos, the internet, and emphasis on self-improvement. When interviewed, people often report feeling socially disconnected and nostalgic for the old days when people knew each other. Perhaps this awareness will be a first step toward a reverse in the trend.

Chapter Five

THE FAMILY

Nearly all Americans have a family somewhere, but it's often far from evident. The lack of strong family ties is one thing that strikes nearly all visitors to America (with the exception of those from Sweden, where apparently the family is even less demanding).

When an American speaks of "my family," he probably means his immediate, nuclear family: the group that lives together in one household – father, mother and children or whatever combination of those remain. The larger family – the grandparents, aunts, uncles and cousins – are often far away. Or even if nearby, they can be a small presence in each other's lives, visiting back and forth very little.

Photo: Marcia Lieberman

The ideal American family. Although these people may see other relatives on holidays, just the four of them feel self-sufficient as a family.

A quarter of American households consist of one person living alone.

There are plenty of exceptions to this configuration: large families that have lived for generations in one town and gather together in all their spare moments, for example. But in the cities and suburbs, each small family is more often floating free of the hometown connections. And to a much greater degree than in many countries, individual members of the family carry on a social life apart from the others.

If you make American friends, you may know them for a long time before meeting their families. Various members of the family with different interests are expected to have different friends. Two women may lunch together or two men might regularly play golf, without ever meeting each other's spouses or children.

"Don't these Americans ever sit down and eat a meal with their families?" asks one Italian woman I know. Yes, many of us do, but according to the statistics, not regularly. Nonetheless, the family remains the entity we fall back on. Holidays, weddings and funerals bring the larger family together, and in times of trouble we turn to our families. But the trail of obligation generally runs only between parents and children. Few people feel much sense of duty to members of the extended family.

Marriage

The couple has to find each other, and it isn't always easy. Marriages are supposed to be between two people who fall in love, but the great complaint of young – and middle-aged – people is that it is hard to meet other "singles." College is a golden opportunity, but after college there are fewer meeting points. Lacking a community life, it is perfectly possible for young working people to simply not meet other eligible people.

At one time, advertising in newspapers or searching for love on the internet was considered an embarrassing last resort. No longer. It's the modern solution and less time-consuming than hanging around in bars. Most communities have local papers with personal ads, and it's even easier to find forums on the internet.

The big online services have their own sites or you can check established sites such as www.match.com or matchmaker.com, or simply search "personals." When you "meet" someone, you begin by exchanging email correspondence. If that goes well, you advance to a telephone call. Finally, you meet, but unless you have limited your search to your local area, you could be required to board an airline flight. Online dating keeps many people up late at night, sitting at their computers. One note of caution: Only meet your dates in public places until you know them very well.

The Couple

Once joined, an American couple expects to be happily married, and to a large degree, they are. One obvious reason for this is the prevalence of divorce. If a couple gets along badly, they do not feel they must spend the rest of their lives together. This was not always so: to have "failed at marriage" was a social stigma thirty years ago, and for this and other reasons more of the unhappily married stayed married. Since then, the American divorce rate has tripled.

The American idea of a well-matched couple (Raymonde Carroll elaborates on this in her brilliant book, *Cultural Misunderstandings*) is one which always presents a united front to the world. Each member of the couple should be highly supportive of the other (in the same manner that "good" parents are supportive, rather than critical, of their children). They are expected to share a number of interests and activities and should spend vacations and weekend evenings together.

In public, the happy couple demonstrates coupleness with affectionate gestures and solicitude. At parties, they will often be found chatting in the same circle. The suspicion that they might not prefer each other's company to all others is cause for concern.

A good many of those who do divorce never remarry. Thus one out of four American households with children is headed by a single adult. (In some of these, the parent never married.) Any foreigners thinking favourably of the American tendency for divorce should note that recent studies suggest that the children suffer long-term disadvantages. On average, they grow up much poorer than those in two-parent families, have less chance of going to college, and are less likely to have satisfactory marriages themselves.

Living Together

In the last thirty years, society has ceased to frown on sexual relations between unmarried adults, and many couples live together without getting married. A minority continue to live together indefinitely without getting married, but most of these arrangements conclude either at the altar (i.e., in marriage) or in dissolution. Most people still want their children to have properly married parents.

Blended Families

The "blended" family occurs when divorced parents remarry, uniting their children into one household. Such families have many inherent problems. The step-parents are often resented and somewhere else the children have another parent, who is frequently on bad terms with his or her former spouse. At best, the children adjust, but the complications of blended families are many.

Housework

The division of housework poses a problem in many American households. Before the Women's Liberation movement, women did nearly all of it while men were expected to take care of the outdoor work – despite the almost total lack of outdoor work in urban households. Now that so many women have jobs, most people agree that housework should be shared. However, old habits die hard. In actual fact, the women still do most of the housework and childcare, although in younger couples the men contribute more than their fathers did.

Babies

Fathers are often present in the delivery room, which has become a more humane place than it used to be. Most people aspire to natural childbirth (that is, with as few drugs as possible), although births still usually take place in hospitals, in case of complications. Some parents now choose to have midwives rather than doctors preside over the delivery.

If all goes well, women leave the hospital very shortly after giving birth. At least half of them breastfeed their babies, feeling that nature's way is best for many reasons. There is no prohibition against

Photo: Marcia Lieberman

"Good" husbands accompany their wives to childbirth classes and are present while the baby is born. They may learn breathing exercises that help their wives relax during delivery.

women leaving the house in the weeks after childbirth, and they may return quickly to their active lives. Women often return to work much sooner than they would care to because most companies do not give long maternity leave.

Professional couples may put off having children until they are in their thirties or even forties and then generally feel that one or two children are enough. The long-awaited baby is much doted on and causes a drastic change in his or her parents' lives. The new parents who formerly went out to dinner nearly every night and saw every new movie stay home and talk baby talk.

Single Parents

At some time or other during their childhoods, half of American children will be living with only one parent, usually a mother. The child may have another loving parent involved in his or her life, but at least according to statistics, the mother is apt to be the sole support. Consequently, this is commonly a poor household. When the mother is a teenager, the odds become daunting that either mother or child will ever escape poverty.

When both parents remain involved in a child's life, there is likely to be a court order determining how much time a child spends with each parent. In some cases, the parents have joint custody and thus are supposed to share the care of the child equally.

Daycare

Just over half of American mothers with children under five years old have jobs. Many go back to work in the first few months of their new babies' lives. As only a quarter of these have mothers, husbands, or other relatives able and willing to look after the baby during the day, finding good childcare has become a giant problem.

The government operates very few daycare centres, and these are reserved for low-income families. A minuscule number of workplaces provide daycare facilities. There are numerous private daycare centres, but the staff is often underpaid and weary from looking after too many children. Few of these accept infants or toddlers who aren't toilet-trained. Cooperative daycare centres have the advantage of high parent supervision, but parents must be able to contribute a certain amount of time each week.

Parents who can afford to will try to hire someone to come into their home and look after the baby, but good caretakers are hard to find and keep. Live-in nannies usually come from foreign countries as such work is not popular among Americans. Sometimes two sets of parents will share one caretaker. Alternatively, the parents may take their child to the home of someone who takes in several children during the day.

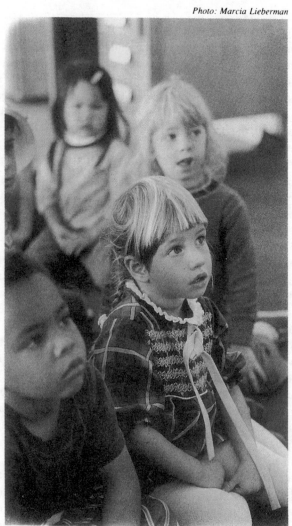

Children too young for school whose parents work often spend their days in "daycare centres" where they are cared for by paid workers.

In recent years, there has been much reporting of sexual and physical abuse in daycare centres. How much of this reporting is accurate and how much abuse really takes place is unknown. At any rate, parents should be extremely careful in selecting a daycare centre. The chances that your child will suffer overt abuse are low, but it is quite possible that your child will receive less loving attention than you would wish. You should be very suspicious of any centre that does not welcome unexpected parental visits or tries to keep the parents at an arm's length from the classrooms.

Babysitters

The whole concept of evening babysitters is a novelty to many foreigners, to whom the thought of leaving children in the care of a stranger is appalling. What would actually be appalling to us is the thought of never being able to get away from the kids. Lacking a supply of relatives to look after our children, we hire someone, which has the added benefit of allowing us to pay for the service and not have to build up any social obligations.

The babysitter might be the older child of neighbours, someone recommended by friends, or a student from a nearby college. If the first time went well, we would try to hire the same babysitter, so he or she won't remain a stranger long. But as long as the person is reliably recommended, we don't worry overly about the stranger aspect, as American children are supposed to learn to relate to many different people.

The usual routine with the babysitter is to, first or all, leave a phone number where you can be reached in case of an emergency, then oral or written instructions for children's bedtime and other rules relating to television, computer games, meals, and an invitation to "help yourself to anything in the refrigerator." You should have established when you first spoke how much you pay per hour (you'll have to find out what local terms usually are). You are responsible for seeing that the babysitter gets home safely – meaning that you either drive him or her home or provide taxi fare.

Bringing Up Children

Foreigners are shocked when they first arrive and hear American children say to their parents things like, "It's none of your business" or "Dad, you're really dumb." However, American parents feel their children have many rights, including freedom of speech. Children are also allowed to make many of their own choices – what to wear, what to watch on television, how to spend their free time, what extra-curricular activities to pursue, and even what school to attend.

This degree of freedom may seem ridiculous to non-Americans, but there are reasons why the upbringing of an American child is quite different from that of a Thai, Chinese, French or Brazilian child. In most other countries in the world, parents feel that their obligation is to raise an obedient child who will fit into society. The little ego must be moulded into that of a well-behaved citizen.

Not so here. Although there are many things a child must learn – from eating with a knife and fork to driving a car – the top priority is to raise an individual capable of taking advantage of opportunity. Such a person cannot be overly obedient or hindered by too many family attachments. American life is marked by change and those who thrive are self-sufficient, quick jumpers who can exist, if need be, far from family. Children are taught to be autonomous rather than to fit into the group.

Self-Discovery

The child must get the chance to find his or her niche. This means leaving him or her free to experiment, to try one thing and then another. We (at least in theory) resist the kind of tracking that in many countries directs children along career paths from a young age. If you're going to fulfil your potential – the object in life here – you can't settle down too early.

We also consider it important not to break a child's spirit. A child who is too demure and obedient will not have the audacity to go far in this society. It takes self-confidence to start your own company, to think of new ways to split atoms, to play in a rock band. So parents try to emphasise the positive. Rather than pointing out to a three-year-old that his picture of a house ought to have a roof, we declare it the most magnificent picture of a house ever and tape it to the refrigerator. We want each child to feel that he is a very special child, with unique, notable abilities. After all, self-promotion goes a long way, even in lieu of talent. America's great humorist Mark Twain wrote with some truth, "All you need in life is ignorance and confidence, and then success is sure."

Privacy and private property are both considered sacrosanct. A child may refuse to allow anyone into his room. It is considered poor behaviour on the part of a parent to read a child's diary or mail without permission. Parents shouldn't be too nosy. It is taken for granted that children will have secrets from their parents.

Many parents do not believe in spanking and will carry on long dialogues with the child about misbehaviour in situations when many foreigners would report, "I smacked him once and he never did it again." Contrary to some rumours, it is not illegal to hit your children in the US, but it is illegal to seriously hurt them. If you beat them badly, you may hear from the police.

Some parents do seem to give their children more freedom and decision-making power than the child actually wants. Sensible parents modulate decision-making according to age, but the attitude that "it's up to you" is much more prevalent here than elsewhere. Learning through failure is the American way. Abraham Lincoln failed at many enterprises before becoming the nation's president.

The Spoiled Child

Ideally, the American system produces self-confident, capable people. However, it doesn't always, and foreign visitors frequently remark that American children are spoiled. It is true that demanding, tyrannical children are not uncommon.

American parents do not have the confidence they once had regarding child raising. During this century, child psychologists, educators and doctors have become the experts on bringing up children. The experts taught that the child's emotional stability should be the chief goal of child raising. Above all, the child had to be convinced that his parents would love him no matter what he did (this was to instill basic self-confidence). The pressure to please Mommy and Daddy considerably lessened.

At the same time, parental ties to community and larger family (and frequently to each other) were breaking down, and so the parents themselves were becoming less secure. They were increasingly unwilling to be authorities, sometimes unpopular ones, in their children's lives. They wanted their children to be their friends. They did not like to say "no."

Photo: Marcia Lieberman

Parents try to give serious attention to their children's thoughts and feelings.

Appliances and urban living have freed children from chores, so schoolwork is their main obligation (and by most standards, there's not much of that). Most parents are loath to impose any hardship on their children. Toys are cheap so in this age of abundance – and smaller families – children have emerged with rooms full of stuff, including computers and personal televisions. If one is inclined to spoil the children, it is very easy to do so, unlike in a society in which the child's labour is needed and toys are few.

The Re-Invention of Discipline

On the positive side, many people of all ages have good relationships with their parents, far friendlier than in cultures in which the parents, often fathers in particular, are remote authorities. But where "spoiling" rather than understanding is the norm, some unpleasant children have emerged: undisciplined, self-centred and unhappy. Recently, the experts have turned around and discovered "limits," concluding that children are happier when they have parents who act like parents and give them rules and structure.

Newcomers to the United States should take heart that more Americans are rejecting total indulgence. If you are "strict," you may be in the minority, but you are not alone. So do not let your children persuade you that all American parents let their children do anything they want.

Television

Many social analysts now think that the television's domination of the American home is a major contribution to social problems. Television rivals family and church as the dispenser of values. Repeated thousands of times a day in advertisements is the message that acquiring stuff is a worthy social goal. It is a message that children easily succumb to, and the longing of even young children for certain brand names is a product of television.

Situation comedies depict children as fearless loudmouths who outsmart their parents, and children often imitate these fictional characters. Even worse, talk shows bring on real people who shamelessly discuss appalling problems. American television content, with some exceptions, is of very poor quality.

Furthermore, television interrupts family conversation. As Marie Winn, author of *The Plug-In Drug*, says, "Family life becomes parallel rather than interactive." Children who watch television are found to have much poorer imaginations than those who don't. Teachers report as well that television watchers have short attention span. Just as television must amuse every second, now the teacher must be fast-paced and entertaining.

Little children do not acquire language skills from television; learning to speak requires real people to speak with. On the contrary, actual neurological damage can result from spending the formative years in front of the television rather than in dialogue and play. Furthermore, the amount of violence on television gives children and their parents a distorted outlook on the world.

If children spend hours per day in the most effortless manner possible – watching television – they cannot be expected to be very good at making a rigorous effort on demand. Thus American children, who can be very bright and intuitive, are often not inclined to applying themselves to doing "hard" stuff, such as learning their multiplication tables or studying spelling words or even reading books. This gives a great advantage to immigrant children who are capable of hard work and thus capture a remarkable number of academic prizes.

I once asked a roomful of immigrants in an English class, who all objected to the low quality of American television programming, why they did not just get rid of the household television. They laughingly admitted that the whole family had become addicted to it. Foreigners sometimes feel that the television's value as an English language teacher overrides its disadvantages, but that seems optimistic, considering the number of people who have the television on all day and still don't speak English well.

Concerned American parents severely restrict their children's television watching. Studies regularly show that the children who watch the least television have the greatest academic and personal success. A small elite in the country have banished television from their homes altogether.

Teenagers

The teenage years are apt to be difficult for Americans. Delightful as it may seem to be on the threshold of total independence, in fact it can be frightening. Teenagers are aware that they have the task of fulfilling their large potential, but nobody can tell them what this potential is. They have a huge number of choices, and although many will be going on to college, they must decide where to go and what to study and, in some sense, who they will choose to be. It is a much more serious time of life for Americans than for some other nationalities, who see it as a last chance for good times before settling down.

Despite their fears – or perhaps because of them – American youngsters frequently cause their parents a lot of trouble during their teenage years. In fact, parents consider themselves very lucky if their teenagers are not extremely difficult. Simply being a teenager is an excuse for antisocial behaviour. "It's his hormones," say the parents. There are responsible and mature teens, but they too will probably withdraw a great deal from the family during the teen years. After all, the goal is that the child should grow into an adult who is psychologically separate from his or her family.

Even an unusually family-centred teenager feels he must resist family activities for his own self-respect. Most would prefer not to be seen in public with their family. Parents will joke about this and usually cooperate. They know that this is a phase that will pass. One theory for the distress among American teenagers is that, while they are no longer children, they have no real function or responsibility in society. Time hangs heavily on their hands while they wait for adulthood.

Parents may give up trying to influence their teenage children altogether. It's the peer group that becomes all-important. Both boys and girls spend hours in front of the mirror and adhere to rigid standards of dress that identify them with certain groups. They would spend all their time with their friends if they could. Popularity is terribly important. They identify themselves with their chosen group through music, clothes, slang and activities – nearly all selected from a world totally alien to the adult world. Nose rings, tattoos and shaved heads provide the kids with cool ways to horrify their parents.

Not all teenagers, of course, are solely absorbed in teen life. There are a heartening number who give their time to good causes, evidence concern for the larger world, and are ethical, imaginative and hardworking. Many teenagers have alert social consciences and are quick to challenge injustice.

Teenagers often have jobs, not because their families are unable to support them, but in order to have spending money. Parents are generally happy to have their children work; it's another sign that the kids are becoming independent, it gives them responsibility and it keeps them out of trouble. Teenagers are usually paid, directly or through a weekly allowance, by their parents for doing chores and often for babysitting younger siblings.

Sex

"Dating" is less in vogue than it once was, and young people spend a lot of social time hanging around in groups of friends of both sexes. However, some teenagers begin to date as early as ages thirteen or fourteen. The extent of the date depends on age and parental pemissiveness, but most parents see no harm in their youngsters pairing off at a young age – as long as the relationship does not

Photo: Esther Wanning

Teenagers are paid by their parents to do chores. the money they earn goes mostly towards entertainment, such as buying CDs and movie tickets.

become too serious. Most children have a curfew by which they are to be home.

A side effect of the sexual revolution was that teenagers began to feel that it was their right, if not their duty, to be having sex. The rate of teen births skyrocketed, and while it is now falling, it remains the highest among Western countries.

However, foreigners should not assume that a date equals sex here in America. The more sensible teenagers are more likely to restrain themselves and see the virtue in doing so, or at least use condoms and be very discriminating about their partners. And the presence of AIDS and other diseases has given further weight to the arguments against teenage sex. In fact, there is now an abstinence movement (largely spearheaded by Christian fundamentalists), which encourages young people to declare their intentions to remain virgins until marriage.

Drugs

The other great threat on parents' minds is drugs. A variety of illegal drugs are widely available, and many teenagers use them. Whether or not drugs are considered "cool" varies in different schools and communities. Besides alcohol, the most widely used drug is marijuana. The usual effect of marijuana is to make the user inarticulate and passive. You can sometimes tell if a person is "higher" by the redness of their eyes.

There are many more teenagers who have tried drugs than who continue to use them. There are a few who become quickly addicted, steal to support their habits, and drop out of school, but these were not generally happy and well-adjusted children in the first place. If your children are doing well and have a loving family, it is highly unlikely that they are going to become drug addicts just because the opportunity presents itself.

The Foreigners' Despair

To many immigrants to America, the worst part of life here is seeing their children bring home American attitudes of disrespect towards their parents. When the Korean father says to his son, "Come home right after school," and the son replies, "You can't make me," it is disheartening, particularly as society does not seem to be on the father's side.

In Korea, the son would never have defied his father. Here, immigrant children soon get a taste of the freedom American children enjoy and want the same. Whether or not they insist on it, the different standards nearly always cause family conflict. "We want to have fun, but our parents just want us to stay home," a Cambodian lamented.

It is inevitable that the children will want to be more like Americans than their parents would want them to be. The teenage world here is a demanding one, and the new immigrants are trying to fit in. It is better if the parents are not too rigidly attached to the way things were done back home. Families may have a painful period of adjustment, yet ultimately the children will probably grow up to appreciate their family's culture and closeness.

One young Chinese immigrant in a language class, asked if she thought Americans were happy, replied "How could they be happy when they don't have their families around them?" Many of the students in the class nodded agreement. Young people who can combine American opportunities with their own family support structure will be well poised for success in America.

The Young Adult

In the 19th century, there were very few fields of work that required a college degree. A heavy dose of professionalism has now crept into our society, and even people applying for middle management positions are required to have a college diploma. An advanced degree is required to demonstrate expertise at anything at all. Consequently, parents gear themselves up to make great sacrifices to see that their children are college educated.

Many young people contribute to their expenses while in college by working. There is no disgrace in holding down some menial job while "getting an education." As a matter of fact, it is a badge of honour to have worked one's way through college.

Moving Out

For economy, young people may live at home during their college years, but for many the college of their choice is a long way from home. After college, they are expected to find apartments of their own, which are often shared with other young people. The fact that their new housing may be far less luxurious than their parents' home is unimportant compared to gaining adult status.

Their careers, or the appeal of a more glittering city, may cause many to move to another city or state, the start of an odyssey that may keep them forevermore at a distance from the family, although they will visit on holidays. Once they have left home and are self-supporting, parents no longer feel much responsibility for them.

In actual fact, today's young people are unlikely to enjoy the job security of the past, but our confidence in the American way remains. We still believe the deserving can and will succeed, without family interference. And because success is defined by achievement, not by family status, parents fear to inhibit the young person's efforts by "handing it to them on a silver platter."

Despite the expectation that a young adult should be independent, it's not as rare now as it was 25 years ago for young adults to be living with a parent. Often, they have moved back in after living elsewhere for a period. Referred to in the media as "boomerang kids," they seem to be sensibly reacting to high rents and simply admitting that they like the comforts of home. As parents rarely regulate their grown children's sex lives any longer, why not? Some parents are pleased to have their children's company and some aren't, but all have probably asked themselves at some time, "Is there something wrong with this kid that he's had to come back home?"

Just the Cash, Please

Many parents do help their grown children with small outlays of cash. While some will contribute to the down payment for a house, they don't feel obliged to. Once they have provided their offspring with a good upbringing and education, their financial responsibilities are at an end (unless there's a grave emergency, such as severe illness). It's now up to the young people to make something of themselves.

Some foreigners find it strange that the tables don't turn at a certain point so that the young people are helping their parents. Unless the children have become immensely rich, there is no social pressure to do so. What's more, on average, today's young adults feel poorer than their parents, who years ago were able to buy houses when they were cheaper and now don't have the expenses of raising children.

Any Roof but the Kids'

Old people tend to spend their days among other old people or alone. The isolation of the old is astounding to many newcomers here. Traditional cultures would never think up such a thing as an old-age home, an establishment made up entirely of unrelated old people and their caretakers.

However, you should not assume that old people are rejected because they're isolated. Whether or not the relationship is a happy one, grown children feel responsible for the care of aging parents (or at least for seeing that they get care). But independence is valued as much by the old as it is by the young. "I never want to be a burden on my children," is a common phrase on the lips of parents. To have to give up one's own home and go live with a son or daughter, subjected to the moods of badly behaved grandchildren, helpless against loud stereos, ever conscious that one is not a contributing member of the household is an unwanted fate.

Even an old-age home is not always considered such a bad lot. Some are awful, but others are gracious and elegant – but expensive. Paying guests know that they are at least of financial worth to the institution, which is better than being a family dependent. The children may even be financing their parents' stay in the institution, but by not having them under their own roof they are graciously according them some remaining autonomy. Just as their parents encouraged them to be independent at a young age, the children are now allowing the parents to be independent. Having finished with child raising, it is felt that the parents deserve to be around their own peer group – other old people – rather than be bothered by young children.

There are a growing number of "retirement communities," which provide apartments in complexes designed just for old people. Many of these are in the balmier climates of the USA. No children are allowed (except as visitors), a rule set to please the old folks, who obviously do not delight in the pitter-patter of young feet as much as sentimentalists would like to think.

Photo: Marcia Lieberman

Old people hope to enjoy their leisure years and many move to the warmer Southern states, such as Florida.

It's the poor (and recent immigrants who haven't acquired American ideas) who are most apt to spend their last years living with family members. The other options appear to be preferable to anyone who can afford them.

There is much talk these days about "the problem of old people in America." Part of the problem is that there are so many of them and in twenty years it is expected there will be many more. Because people are living to be so much older, many 60-year-olds with heart diseases of their own are concerned about parents in their eighties. Modern medicine has become fairly skilled at keeping very old people alive, but it has not necessarily succeeded at making them healthier. The result is that a large proportion of the country's medical care goes to people in their last years of life. Americans are peculiarly averse to dying, so most die in hospitals while trying to prolong life at all cost.

Pets

It sometimes seems that the most popular member of a family is the family dog. Considering how loyal, polite and affectionate dogs are, this is not surprising. (Americans find the thought of eating dogs repugnant.) Cats are also full-fledged members of many families. When the pet dies, the family is genuinely grief-stricken.

Some foreigners consider it rather a dirty habit to have pets around the house. Indeed, animals do shed hair and bring dirt in on their feet, but they do not carry life-threatening diseases to humans. Most of us (excepting farmers) consider that our cats and dogs belong inside the

Photo: Kristy MacDonald

Dogs are important members of many households.

81

house with the rest of the family. A sure way to infuriate your neighbours is to leave a dog barking outside. Not only will this make you unpopular, you may soon have the sheriff at your door. In most communities, there are laws against barking dogs.

Friends as Family

There are numerous people who claim, "My friends are my family." These people very likely have, somewhere, a real family, but they feel much closer to their friends. American life changes greatly between generations. Parents who live in a Boston suburb, attend the Congregational Church, and have steak cookouts may not know what to make of a vegetarian daughter living on the West Coast who periodically visits her guru in India.

Less drastic differences than this cause alienation in families. Distance alone may account for loss of contact. Instead of family, groups of friends may get together for Thanksgiving and Christmas, go on trips together, and share joys and sorrows. This is particularly true for those who are single, whether before or after being married.

Despite the appeal of replacing an inconvenient family with carefully selected friends, there is a drawback: Friends cannot be expected to proffer as much aid as family. Those who claim to rely on their friends usually are highly independent, with good health and sound finances. Even the best of friends may be keeping track of favours. Your sorrows are not their sorrows. In catastrophe, you are on your own and will probably turn to your real family. No matter how distant the family in America has become, it has not been replaced.

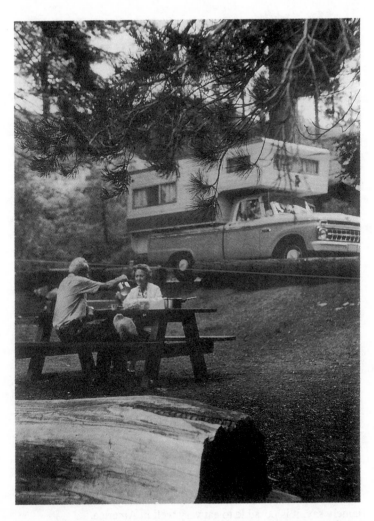

Americans like to roam. Some retired people spend many months of the year living in their recreational vehicles, traveling from campground to campground, constantly socializing with different people.

Chapter Six

DAILY LIFE

FOOD

American cuisine in itself is not bad. Our cooks have an abundance of fresh ingredients and a heritage of wonderful regional dishes: apple pie, clam chowder, southern fried chicken, Louisiana gumbo, barbecued oysters, fresh buttered corn, buttermilk biscuits, strawberry shortcake, and hundreds of other fine dishes. As many guidebooks lamely say, it is possible to eat very well in America.

It is also possible to eat very badly, and many Americans do – by choice rather than necessity. A lot of supermarket food, while cheap and plentiful, is produced to provide the most calories with the longest shelf life and the shortest preparation time. The result is frozen dinners, packaged sweets, instant puddings, bottled salad dressings, and canned sauces. Manufacturers are working night and day to invent new products that will captivate the public. Almost any conceivable meal is available ready-made.

The problem is that most of this stuff isn't much good. It supplies calories, but in real satisfaction it doesn't measure up to anything fresh or home-cooked. Even fruits and vegetables are raised to survive long shipping or storage periods, rather than for taste. Meats are tender and good (unless you like a gamey taste), but very fatty and distressingly laden with hormones and antibiotics. Also, most supermarket food is wrapped, canned, frozen, jarred, or packaged in such a way that you can't examine it until you take it home. (Many are so well sealed that they're maddeningly difficult to open even at home!) If you do try to open jars or poke into packages at the supermarket, the management will be distressed.

If you come from a country with severe food shortages, you won't complain, but most foreigners find American food takes some getting used to. And some searching for the gold among the dross.

Sweet and Bland

A Tanzanian said he found American food so bland he nearly starved when he first came. "Back then, I couldn't even find a bottle of Tabasco (a hot sauce) in my little town." Then he discovered pizza and survived. The American palate has become braver than it used to be, but in the average household you won't find much seasoning in use beyond salt and pepper.

And sugar. There seems to be no end to the march on sweetness. One food writer swears that at a banquet he attended he was served a cup of M&M's (little chocolate candies) as an appetizer. Americans are stuck on sugar, and sugar of some kind (such as "fructose" or "sucrose") is added to most packaged foods. It's hard to find a snack that isn't sweet, and even some main course dishes are served with a sweet, such as pancakes with maple syrup and lamb with mint jelly. American pastries are very sweet, and Americans eat sweet desserts much more regularly than most other peoples.

A lot of sodium (an element in salt) is regularly added to packaged foods, which has caused such an outcry among doctors (too much is said to be bad for the heart) that new lines of foods are coming out advertising themselves as "sodium-free." There are also a lot of sugar-free foods, but you have to read labels carefully to make sure you aren't just getting honey or corn syrup or an awful-tasting artificial sweetener.

A law requires the contents of foodstuffs to be listed on the package, in the order of the greatest to the least quantity. It's enlightening reading. However, there is no requirement, as in many other countries, to label genetically modified organisms (GMOs) – foods with genes from other organisms added to their DNA. If you want to avoid these, you must search for "organic" foods.

Eating Habits

The first two meals of the day eaten by an American are generally quick. The classic American breakfast of bacon and eggs is seen more on weekends than when the whole family is rushing to school or work. Cereal with milk and a cup of coffee is probably the usual morning sustenance of the average American. Lunch consists of a sandwich, soup or salad. Dinner is the large meal of the day. (When the lunchtime meal is the big one it can also be called "dinner," and when the evening meal is simple, it may be called "supper.")

The American dinner has fallen under medical disapproval due to its high cholesterol content. The meal typically consists of a large piece of meat, ketchup, vegetables with butter, potatoes (fried or with butter), and a sweet dessert. It might also be an equally fatty frozen meal, heated in the microwave oven, a high-calorie pizza or a bucket of Kentucky Fried Chicken.

A large proportion of Americans report that they would like to change their diets, but habits are hard to break. The beans, vegetables, and whole grains that doctors keep urging us to eat require time to cook, which we haven't got. Take-out Chinese food is many people's *idea of a low-calorie, low-cholesterol meal, but actually our Chinese restaurants use a lot of fat in their dishes.*

Snacking

There appear to be people who rarely eat a whole meal at once. Instead, they just grab a snack when hungry – a hot dog, a doughnut, a container of sweetened yogurt. At home, they snack while standing in front of the open door of the refrigerator.

What seems to distress our foreign visitors about snacking is the lack of seriousness about food. For people who invest a great deal of time thinking about mouthwatering dishes shared with friends and family, the life of a snacker hardly seems worth living. To us, it's a life rich in efficiency, pared down to the essential elements. If only we could speed up sleeping.

Good Eating

There is, thankfully, another side to this story. Dismayed by a landscape of tasteless fast foods, a reaction has sprung up. It began with the appearance of health food stores, which stock foods in as close to their natural states as possible – wholewheat flour and breads, organic produce (fruits and vegetables grown without chemical fertilizers, pesticides or GMOs), and wide assortments of nuts, beans, and grains.

The health food trend has come to supermarkets, and now some large chains carry eggs from uncaged chickens, peanut butter without additives, organic vegetables, etc. Once the customers materialised, specialty farms started to produce lovingly grown, tasty vegetables and even "organic" cattle and pigs. (Most American meats come from factory farms, in which tens of thousands of animals are cruelly crammed into cages and eat unnatural foods that fatten them quickly. The crowding and stress lead to heavy use of antibiotics. Fish too are now crammed into aquatic "farms," fed, and dosed with drugs.)

Recent Asian and Middle Eastern immigrants have improved the quality of produce markets, and gourmet food stores and fresh fish markets have proliferated. Major cities have grocery stores selling staples for every kind of cuisine. It is possible to find excellent ingredients in most parts of the country, although it may take extra effort and money.

Foodies

There have always been some American gourmets, who take great pleasure in good food. The newest, trendiest version of these are known as "foodies." Foodies are exacting about everything that passes their lips. They are on a voyage of discovery, constantly on the lookout for new and exotic foods: baby beets, sun-dried tomatoes, varieties of mushrooms, salsas, tiramisu. Cheeses alone absorb vast quantities of their attention. They eat only baby lettuce and fresh pasta. They watch famous chefs on television, cook, and explore new restaurants. They do not touch fast food.

Because of the time and financial investment required of foodies, most are Yuppies (Young Upwardly Mobile Professionals) or Dinks (Double Income No Kids). Foodies are exceptions to most of the rules about American eating. They are an influential minority.

DINING OUT

Restaurant dining is not the natural heritage of the American, and constant eating out strikes us as somewhat lazy and thriftless. Nonetheless, as kitchen time disappears, restaurants are increasingly where Americans eat. In large cities you can partake of nearly any cuisine in the world; a small town may have a single diner.

The following categories start with the cheap and end with the high-priced.

Fast Food

Fast food establishments, such as McDonald's, Burger King, Wendy's, KFC (Kentucky Fried Chicken), Subway, Pizza Hut, and Taco Bell purvey their specialties from coast to coast (and around the globe), totalling 300,000 fast-food restaurants nationwide. Their foods are convenient, predictable, cheap, fattening, and according to a recent lawsuit, addictive. (The argument is that their heavy doses of fats and sugars work on the opiod centers of the brain in much the same way drugs do.) A lawsuit is attempting to hold the fast-food corporations responsible for diseases of obesity.

Each item in a fast-food restaurant is mass produced according to an exact prescription. The menu, often illustrated, is permanently displayed above the counter. No alcohol is served. Your food comes with an almost equal weight of plastic and paper serving containers and cutlery, which you are expected to throw into the trash when you're finished. You should specify if you want your order to take out. No tipping is expected.

Coffee Shops

"Coffee shop" may be in the name, and it may not. A coffee shop is easily identifiable, however, by its seating arrangements (a counter, booths, and possibly some tables) and bright lighting. You needn't wait to be seated. In the classic coffee shop, waitresses call you "Honey," and pies and doughnuts are displayed in glass cases behind the counter.

Sandwiches are the mainstay of the menu, although a short-order cook stands over the grill and turns out eggs, pancakes, burgers, and fries. Occasionally a coffee shop will have a dinner menu, but most aren't even open for dinner. The breakfasts are usually an excellent bargain. (Americans like going out for breakfast, especially on weekends.)

A waitress will often offer coffee as soon as you sit down. In the hospitable western part of the country, she will refill your coffee cup

Photo: Esther Wanning

Distinctive little eateries such as this may be well worth stopping at. You are likely to find real people and real food. This particular one, in the state of Maine, features seafood and blueberry dishes.

as fast as you can empty it. On the East Coast (where "regular" means with cream), you will have to pay for your second and third cups of coffee. However, you may find that one cup is more than enough as coffee shop coffee is not highly rated.

You may be able to order beer or wine in a coffee shop, but rarely hard liquor. Often you pay a cashier on the way out. You should leave a tip of about 15% on the table because it won't be included on the bill.

For really good coffee, you go to a café, such as Starbucks. These serve expensive espresso drinks and usually fancy pastries and delicacies, rather than hearty food.

Diners

Diners are the rural version of the coffee shop. They do their best to look like railroad passenger cars, and you should not shun one merely because it looks a little rundown on the outside. The food may be excellent, unlike the fast-food franchise which always looks newly minted. Legend has it that you tell a good diner by the number of big trucks parked in front of it – truck drivers are supposed to know where they'll get their money's worth, although it may be that their choice is based on the size of the parking lot instead. Still, a truck stop may be colourful and probably will be cheap.

Family Restaurants

This is an amorphous category, so-called because you can bring the kiddies, usually meaning the place is fairly casual, the bar, if any, is out of sight, a high chair is available for the baby and the food is of the familiar American kind – chops, steaks, fried fish, salads, and potatoes. (The "family," however, does not include your dog, who is barred from all restaurants by sanitary codes.) Many family restaurants are Italian, and pizza and spaghetti now seem as American as apple pie.

On entering, you should wait to be seated. No matter how crowded the restaurant is, you won't be asked to share a table with another party, even if you're alone. If you spy a table you prefer to the one you're led to, feel free to speak up.

You'll probably get a basket of bread and a glass of water without asking. Menus are frequently large and elaborate, describing the food in superlatives ("cooked-to-perfection chicken breasts in Bèchamel cream sauce with fresh seasonal vegetables"), but you should ignore the adjectives when deciding what to order.

You may have a choice of ordering a dinner or à la carte. If you order à la carte, you will be paying separately for the various components of your meal, such as the salad and dessert. The dinner, which costs more, includes the extra courses. Read the small print to find out what comes with what.

At this level of dining you may run into one of the new chummy waiters. Such a one will appear at your table and say, "Hello. How are you tonight? My name is Steve. I'm going to be your waiter. I'd like to tell you about our specials." (If he doesn't tell you the price of the specials, be sure to ask.) You are not expected to introduce yourselves to him. After his speech is over, he will behave much more like a real waiter – disappearing when you want him most – than a friend. When you want to call him, you do not hiss or snap your fingers as in some countries. You must try and catch his eye.

Your soup or salad will be served before the main course. Presumably this is to keep you happy while you're waiting. The drawback is that after bread and salad one is often too full to eat the rest of the meal. As large servings are a feature of family-style restaurants, you may want to ask for a "doggie bag" to take your leftovers home in. The waiter will whisk your plate away and bring back your dinner wrapped up for your next day's lunch.

Family restaurants have a pleasant lack of pretension and reasonable prices, but do not attract gourmet eaters. A 15% tip is sufficient, as in most restaurants.

The Ethnic Restaurants

In the big cities, you have your choice, from Afghani to Zimbabwean, with prices big and little. The Asian selection has particularly exploded in recent years, and in many of these a little money goes a long way. In the Southwest and California, there are also many wonderful Mexican and other south-of-the-border restaurants. In Middle America, Chinese may be your only choice when the urge for something foreign comes over you.

Regional Restaurants

Keep your eye out for regional specialties when you're travelling around the country. In the South you can hope to find hominy grits, black-eyed peas, mustard greens, southern fried chicken, sweet potato pie, okra soup, and numerous other specialties. (The South has some wonderful cafeterias you might want to try; most cafeterias in the North are of low quality.)

New England is known for corn, clam, and fish chowder, New England Boiled Dinner (corned beef and boiled vegetables), Boston baked beans, and blueberry pie. In Louisiana, Creole specialties are blackened fish, shrimp gumbo, and Creole pralines. The West goes in for barbecued meats of any kind, corn-on-the-cob, baked trout, and bean soup. However, don't expect to automatically find New England specialties in New England restaurants, western specialties in the West, etc. You will probably have to search them out.

Bar Restaurants

Some of the better food is found in places where much drinking is done. It won't be fancy, but simple steaks and large sandwiches are often excellent and not overpriced. You do want to take the noise factor into consideration.

Trendy Restaurants

Trendy restaurants are the ones talked about, and "foodies" hasten to every new one. In many of these places, the chef dreams up original dishes, often marrying unexpected cuisines together. Novelty is often what makes a restaurant trendy. In California, one of the trendiest new restaurants serves only raw, vegan food – but elegantly prepared in beautiful surroundings. Certain regional cuisines periodically become trendy. Down-home comfort foods – such as meatloaf, stuffed cabbage, and mashed potatoes – have enjoyed a renaissance lately. Often notable for stunning, expensive décor, very trendy restaurants may play alarmingly loud and awful music by way of suggesting that they are fun places.

Haute Cuisine

The peak dining experiences in America are often in the French restaurants. This is also where you'll find the most intimidating level of service – captains, tuxedoed waiters, sommeliers, busboys, and so on. It is best to have an expense account and to know bits of French in order to read the menu.

You will need to make a reservation, by phone, in advance. If you don't arrive reasonably on time (within 15 minutes or so), you may not get a table. Some restaurants enjoy such popularity that they are booked weeks in advance.

There is a lot of rigmarole to eating in these places, and many Americans feel a bit insecure about protocol in them. When the waiter uncorks the wine, he will pour a little bit into the glass of whoever ordered it. This person is to taste it, and then nod approvingly, perhaps adding "very good," whereupon the waiter will serve the other members of the party.

You are only supposed to refuse the wine if it's actually not fit to drink – not because you have just discovered that you don't like that particular wine. This will only expose you as ignorant.

When the check comes, you should study the items and addition before paying. This is a very respectable thing to do, and you may be sure that even Rockefellers (the legendary rich American family) take care that they are not being overcharged.

Waiters in these grand places expect 20% tips (very rarely is a tip already added to the bill); there's a place on the credit card receipt for adding a tip. Calculate the tip on the pre-tax charge. Do not worry about tipping the many different individuals who served you, unless you had some special service, such as a maître d' who found you a table when you hadn't reserved one. A cloakroom attendant should be tipped a dollar per coat.

Not every French restaurant is so formal, and there are now plenty of other kinds of restaurants vying with the French ones for the top dollars; high-class Italian and "continental" (eclectic European) achieve similar degrees of elegance and price.

DRINKING

Although Americans are consuming less alcohol than ever before, drinking still occupies a large role on the social stage. "Let's meet for a drink" usually means let's get together at a bar after work and before dinner, although such a thing can also be done after dinner.

Some bars serve food, but their primary stock is alcohol. The price of a drink could vary from $2.00 in a down-and-out saloon to $14.00 in a mahogany-panelled room with a view. You won't get a menu, but the bartender is supposed to know how to make almost any concoction you order. Mixed drinks (known as cocktails when consumed before dinner) have ringing names that suggest little about the ingredients: Martinis, Margaritas, Cosmopolitans, Bloody Mary's, Cement Mixers, B-52s. Many of them pack a wallop so it's wise to find out what you're imbibing. You may also order whisky neat (no ice), on the rocks (with ice), or in a highball (with ice and water in a tall glass).

Don't let it worry you if you don't happen to drink. Many people do not and go right on "meeting for drinks." Soda water or tonic with lime are non-drinker standards, and every bartender can make a Virgin Mary – spicy tomato juice without the vodka of a Bloody Mary.

In some bars, you pay for your first round with a large bill, then leave the change on the counter. The bartender will remove the correct amount from the pile for each subsequent round. You pocket what's left when you've finished, leaving a tip.

After a few drinks, you do not wish to casually wander the streets of any large American city late at night. Be sure you know where you are and how you're getting home. And don't accept a ride from a friend who has had one drink too many.

TABLE MANNERS

When to Eat

Back on the farm, where the day started at 4 a.m., dinner was at 5 p.m. Our dinner hour remains quite early, although family dinners have gotten later since Mom got a job.

A. Cutting with the knife and fork. One cuts only a few bites at a time.

B. Taking a bite: fork in action. Note that the eater leans slightly forward but does not slump over her plate.

C. The mouth closes daintily around the food. The diner continues to face her companion directly.

D. Eating soup, which the diner pours into her mouth from the side of the soup spoon.

E. When she senses that her lips are wet with food, the diner delicately wipes her mouth with her napkin.

F. This arrangement of knife and fork indicates to the waiter that the diner has not finished eating.

G. The arrangement of knife and fork here signals that the waiter may remove the plate.

Photos: Kristy MacDonald

D

E

F

G

You might meet someone at a restaurant any time between 6 and 8 p.m., but rarely later, unless travelling in very sophisticated circles. The East Coast operates at somewhat later hours than the West, partly because people on the West Coast have to get up early in the morning to call people on the East Coast.

Breakfast takes place before the day's work begins, whenever that is. Noon is the classic lunch hour, although many people eat earlier or later – largely to escape the crowds. Few people take more than an hour for lunch, unless there's a business excuse for it.

The Mechanics of Eating

Correctly, no one should start eating until everyone has been served. However, if some people are served before others, the unserved should turn to the served and say, "Don't wait; please start." The served pretend to do so, but pick slowly at their food until everyone can eat.

The array of silverware at a classy dinner can be formidable, but the rule is simple: use it from the outside in. That is, you use the outside spoon for your soup, the middle one for dessert, and the inner one for your coffee. The truth is, though, that nobody will notice or care if you use the salad fork for your cake.

We eat nearly everything with a fork, which most right-handed people hold in the right hand. If something has to be cut up, you switch your knife to the right hand, do your cutting (holding the item in place with the fork in the left hand), then lay down the knife (on the side of the plate), switch the fork back to the right hand, stab the bite-sized piece with the fork and eat. Got it? There are those (English people in particular) who ridicule our mode, preferring the efficiency of keep-ing the fork in the left hand and the knife in the right.

You use the fork even when facing a number of foods that easily could be eaten with the fingers. Generally, if something could grease up your fingers, don't touch it. The exception is fried chicken, which may be seized between both hands. Bread, bacon, artichokes, pizza, olives, corn-on-the-cob, and raw vegetables may be eaten with the fingers. With rolls and muffins, we break off and butter one small piece at a time, having first transferred an adequate supply of butter from the general butter plate to our own butter plate. Never stick your hand or your fork into a serving dish. If you want the last cherry tomato left in the salad bowl, remove it to your plate with the salad tongs.

When the knife is not in action, it is most pleasing to have the free hand resting in the lap, although few people will look askance at a forearm on the table. The eating arm should rise off the table when carrying food to the mouth; the mouth must not be lowered to meet the fork or spoon. One leans forward slightly to avoid drips in one's lap. Elbows are properly kept off the table, at least until the plates are cleared. Implements should not be waved around in the air to punctuate conversation.

Foods too liquid to be eaten with a fork are eaten with a spoon: soup, ice cream, puddings. It is bad form to drink from your soup bowl, which should not be lifted from the table. The soup spoon is slightly larger than a dessert or coffee spoon, and you pour its contents into your mouth from its side, not from the tip. When you're finished, lay the spoon on the plate under the soup bowl. You indicate that you've finished your main course by laying the knife and fork side-by-side on the right-hand side of the plate.

You should not burp or slurp at the table, although blowing one's nose is perfectly all right. (Persistent sniffling is irritating.) Do not pick your teeth. Food should slide into your mouth as quietly as possible, then be chewed with the mouth closed. Most Americans are put off by the sight of the food in someone else's mouth. You must swallow your food before speaking or at least give the appearance of having done so. Should someone suddenly ask if you realise that your wife is having an affair, you must still finish chewing before replying.

The Check

My Chinese friend was dumbfounded to hear of a father and two brothers who went out to dinner and split the check three ways. I assured him that this was most unusual in a family, but among friends, splitting the check is common. Unless it was made very clear to you that someone else is paying – or you are – you should expect to pay your share of the check.

If you're with friends, and someone else grabs the check and says, "Here, I'll get this," you might protest, but you can generally assume the other person genuinely means to pay. If you really don't want him or her to, you can try to force a bill over, saying, "Here, at least take this."

A frequent question is whether to simply split the check in equal shares or have each person pay for precisely what he or she ate. The person who says, "Let's just split it, shall we?" should not be the one who consumed most extravagantly. So if you ordered filet mignon and insisted on champagne, you should pay more.

This exactitude horrifies many foreigners, but it represents not so much stinginess on our part as our fondness for self-reliance and our idea of fairness. If you don't owe me and I don't owe you, we have a nice even relationship (which I may be willing to sacrifice in favour of a free meal, but if I really doubt that you can afford to pick up the check, I will be embarrassed if you insisted on paying).

Smoking Sections

In many places, smoking in restaurants is banned. In others, restaurants are required to provide both smoking and non-smoking sections, and the hostess will ask you which you would prefer. When this question comes up, smokers do not automatically defer to nonsmokers. If yours is a mixed party, you will just have to try to work out your seating in the way that will cause the least all-round suffering.

FREEDOM FROM DIRT

Home and Person

"Cleanliness is next to godliness," my grandmother used to say. Americans are almost religious in their devotion to eliminating dirt. Daily baths or showers are the norm, underwear and socks are changed daily, and men head out the door each morning in a fresh shirt.

In fact, it has been shown that the American housewife spends more time doing housework than she did fifty years ago. One reason is that standards of cleanliness have risen to meet the time saved by washing machines and vacuum cleaners. A great deal of effort can go into making kitchen floors and counters shine; supermarkets fill entire aisles with cleaning formulas and devices.

Most important of all, the American person does not wish to smell dirty. The matter is so sensitive that hardly anyone will tell someone who smells badly the truth. An enormous industry produces deodorants, aftershave lotions, powders, and colognes guaranteed to fend off any hint of body odour. A person who vigorously exercises will want to shower immediately afterwards. Houses now often have as many or more bathrooms as occupants, each a sparkling temple to cleanliness.

The Streets

On a world scale, American cities aren't too dirty, but they don't compete with Copenhagen or Tokyo. We do not like garbage-strewn streets, and the better suburbs are immaculate, with perfectly cut lawns and not an ice cream wrapper in sight. In many poor city neighbourhoods, on the other hand, trash blows around freely, and graffiti defeats fresh-paint efforts.

Under no circumstances should you drop waste, be it ever so small, on the ground. Practically every community has some sort of public trash collection, but we are a civic-minded people and consider

101

everyone responsible for keeping the outdoors tidy. If there is no trash can in sight, you may have to fill your pockets with empty bottles and candy wrappers until you get home. Good citizens go so far as to pick up other people's refuse when they're in a park or garden.

The rule goes for the middle of the desert, the national parks, zoos, and mountain tops as well. Those who offend nature by leaving refuse behind are considered to have had poor upbringing. Alas, there are many of them, despite fines for littering. In a country like ours, which generates such mountains of waste, one considers with horror where general littering would lead.

Noise Pollution

As might be expected in a country settled by Pilgrims, Puritans, and Quakers, we don't like unnecessary noise. We can stand the sounds of progress such as jackhammers and chainsaws, but we do not feel our neighbour has the right to disturb our peace.

At any rate, this is the opinion of the old guard. Unfortunately, our neighbour now has the means at his disposal – namely stereos with incredible decibel levels – to disturb us from blocks away. Since popular music has come to rely on volume to impose its message, a generation has grown up that seems to equate silence with death. But it should not be thought that because some excuse for music is everywhere, filling elevators and offices, that everybody loves it. Primarily it is the idea of youth to live in a world where the music never stops, and, as many foreigners have observed, the power of youth has gotten out of hand in the USA. Sometimes it seems that only very expensive restaurants will let you dine in peace.

Noise and the Law

Despite the inroads of the noisy, the law is generally on the side of the peaceful. Each community has its own noise code, regulating volumes at certain times of day and night. If your neighbours continuously disturb you with noisy parties, you can probably get satisfaction by calling the police – and many people do (to the horror of my friend from El Salvador who can't imagine doing such a thing to one's neighbours). Driving around blasting a car stereo is strictly illegal in most cities, although police are usually more preoccupied with other matters. Working car mufflers are also required.

If you have neighbours whose television or stereo disturbs you, you should not be embarrassed to ask them to turn it down. You will be performing a community service. One is often successful in requesting a reduction of musical volume in restaurants.

Some suburban areas have banned the use of leaf blowers because their roar filled every weekend. If you find yourself in a back yard community, you might consider what you can do to preserve the quiet. The soothing click-click of a manual lawn mower is much more pleasant than the roar of a gas-powered one.

Theatres, Concerts, Churches

There are countries where chatter by members of the audience does not cause offence, but this isn't one of them. Here, any movement of the lips during a concert or a church service is thought to be too much. Also no unwrapping of cough drops, excessive coughing (leave if you must), cracking of joints, chewing gum, foot-tapping, jingling jewellery, or undue fidgeting. Or at least this is the ideal. In fact, many Americans are too restless to sit quietly through anything, to the distress of those who hold to the old standards.

The rules for the movies are slightly less strict than those at high culture events, but still commentary should not extend beyond a whispered, "I' ll be right back." Noisy unwrapping of candy bars, etc., will produce dirty looks from those around you.

SMOKING

Smoking is very much out of fashion in the United States. As soon as smoke from other people's cigarettes ("second-hand smoke") was proven unhealthy, the non-smokers drew battle lines. There is now a ban on radio and television advertising of cigarettes. Smoking is prohibited on all airline flights within – and most flights to and from – the continental United States. Ordinances have passed in many locales banning all smoking in public buildings. Many restaurants have smoking and nonsmoking sections. Some companies don't allow smoking; others have incentive programs to get their employees to quit. In some states, workplace safety ordinances prohibit smoking nearly everywhere, including in bars.

A smoker may reach for a cigarette with some embarrassment. It is generally assumed that he is someone who has tried to quit and failed; by smoking he reveals some flaw in his personality. If you wish nonetheless to smoke, first make sure you're doing it in a place where smoking is allowed. Do not ever light up in an elevator (fire regulations prohibit it).

If you're in someone's home or office and feeling a craving for a cigarette, you might ask, "Is there anywhere I can smoke?" Your hosts will either tell you to go ahead and light up and will find you an ashtray or will point to the street or back yard. House guests of nonsmokers may spend a good deal of time shivering in the garden.

Pipe smoking is slightly more acceptable than cigarette smoking, but pipe smokers should still inquire before lighting up. Outside of the new cigar clubs, cigar smoking is wholly unacceptable – unless you and your host are alone smoking cigars together.

DRIVING

An international driver's license, available at American Automobile Association (AAA) offices, is a desirable item to have, but not absolutely required for visitors. However, the police would much rather deal with one than something in, say, Arabic, and so would rental car companies. You must get an American driver's license after a year's residence here, which requires passing both a written and a driver's test. Even if your stay won't be that long, it's a good idea to pick up a booklet on driving rules at the state motor vehicle bureau.

Traffic laws are taken seriously here. While it's true that on some highways marked at 55 miles per hour the traffic may be moving at 65 miles per hour, the argument that "everybody was doing it" will not help you in court. You must come to a complete stop at red lights and stop signs, even if there isn't another car in sight (the one you don't see may be a police car).

If a police car wants to stop you, he will follow you flashing his overhead lights. Even if you can't imagine what's on his mind, pull over. You should remain in your car, with your driver's license and car registration ready. You may also need to produce proof of car insurance.

Parking regulations are enforced as well, and fines can be high. It is particularly dispiriting to find that one's car has been towed away and can only be retrieved at great cost. You will have to find out what the various curb colours and signs in different communities indicate. Never park in front of a fire hydrant or at a bus stop. In most states, you may make a right turn on a red light, traffic permitting.

Do not attempt to bribe a policeman. The gesture will not be appreciated, and happily, corruption among them in most regions is low. You might do better trying to persuade one that your foreignness accounted for your confusion. If you feel you have been unfairly cited, you may appear in traffic court and argue your case.

HAZARDS

Crime

Few people arrive here unaware of American crime. It is so well publicised that many foreigners are surprised to find that there isn't a bandit behind every tree. Although there is indeed a high crime rate – which inhibits us all – the odds are that the visitor will not have any personal experience with it.

In fact, the US murder rate has been sharply declining since 1991, and a high proportion of murders take place in very poor neighbourhoods or in criminal circles. Unless you're smuggling drugs, your odds of getting murdered are slight. Nonetheless, Americans are cautious walking in certain areas; there are districts of some cities that I would not set foot in under any circumstances.

Robbery rates have also declined, but people still bolt their doors and set up burglar alarms – even in safe suburbs. We are a rather fearful people and don't care to take chances with our health or safety.

The Problem

A large proportion of crime is in some way related to illegal drugs. Drug use is widespread; users may be successful professionals, the alienated offspring of middle class families, or poor people, enviously watching on television the ritzy lives of the successful.

The most visible drug use is in the ghettos (city areas of much crime, little family stability, high unemployment) among hopeless young people. Drug use dissolves moral inhibitions and drugs are high-priced, so brutal crimes for money result.

The crime problem is exacerbated by the millions of guns floating around the country. It is an amazing fact that almost anyone can go into a store and buy a handgun – or a semi-automatic machine gun.

A phrase in the United States Constitution granting the "right to bear arms" causes the National Rifle Association to insist that any limitation on gun sales is unconstitutional. Actually, the founding fathers were providing protection against unpopular tyrants and probably would have considered the free sales of hand guns as crazy as most foreigners do.

Precautions

Foreigners are automatically more vulnerable to crime than natives because they're on unfamiliar territory. They are less aware of what trouble feels like, less wary of the suspicious character. They pause when they should be walking briskly and stare at the tops of buildings when they should be looking at doorways.

Here are a few precautions:

- Keep your wits about you . When you're on city streets, don't ever get so lost in rapture that you are not conscious of your surroundings. People who look lost in any manner are easy targets.

- In American cities, bad areas and good ones can be intermixed in a manner perilous to the stroller. If you're a visitor, have someone tell you which areas to avoid. If you suddenly find yourself in an uncomfortable area, leave, hailing a taxi if necessary.

- Don't ever become separated from your pocketbook. You should have body contact with it at all times in public. Even in a restaurant, be sure you've stowed it where no one can snatch it.

- Men's wallets are best in a sealed pocket. Lacking that, the front pants pocket or inside jacket pocket is best. Be on the lookout for anyone who jostles you in a crowd. (Sometimes he's just distracting you while his accomplice picks your pocket.)

- Don't carry around any more cash than you need. Nearly every purchase can be made with a credit card, and travellers' checks can provide cash reserves. The Japanese, who are not accustomed to paying for meals with credit cards and often carry large amounts of cash, are known to thieves as fine targets.

- Always lock your car. Put possessions in the trunk rather than visibly on car seats. If you're travelling with a carload of stuff, be careful where you park. At night, bring bags into your motel or hotel. In some areas you don't ever want to leave things in the trunk. People in New York City go so far as to put signs in their car windows, saying, "Thieves, don't bother. Radio already stolen."

- In hotels, have your valuables locked in the safe.

- Keep your eyes on your luggage at the airport. Airports are well worked by thieves, and foreigners are first-choice victims.

- Don't go to a park at night – unless there's some sort of event going on.

- If someone does "mug" you (threaten you with harm unless you turn over your money), give him your money. Far better to lose your money than to be hurt.
- Always lock hotel room, apartment, and house doors. Do not open the door unless you know who is on the other side. Many doors have a peephole so you can look through and see for yourself.
- If you open a window, check to make sure it doesn't provide easy access to an intruder. Close windows before going out.
- Have your keys ready before you walk into your building. If you are entering a locked apartment building, do not allow anyone to slip in with you. If you are entering the foyer of your building and think someone is following you, walk on down the street until you've lost the person.
- If you are robbed, call 911, the police emergency number. You do not pay the police for coming.
- Obey the police and don't make sudden moves around them. They have guns and will shoot if threatened.

Drugs

Illegal drugs have been a problem for a long time among the have-nots of America. Heroin (made from the poppy and imported from Asia and Latin America) has created drug addicts and caused crime for years. Marijuana has been long available in some inner city neighbourhoods, but it was not until the 1960s that college students widely indulged in smoking marijuana. Since then, marijuana has become much stronger and its use has spread around the country. And the use of a wide variety of illegal drugs has spread into every level of society. Heroin addiction has become a major problem among middle-class youth.

Marijuana, which comes from an easily grown plant, makes the user feel dreamy and confused, passive rather than violent. For people who are "stoned" a lot, problems don't get solved, the laundry doesn't get washed, appointments aren't met. Its use is particularly unfortunate among young people who don't face the problems of growing up. It is a dangerous drug for a worker who must be alert. Fortunately, not everybody likes the effects of marijuana. Some people feel paranoid when they smoke it or unpleasantly weird.

Cocaine is popular among young, urban professionals because besides producing a fine feeling of wellbeing, it makes the user feel creative and energetic. However, the euphoria lasts but a short time, it's expensive, and people who become addicted are subject to some unpleasant physical side effects. Clinics are now full of people trying to kick the cocaine habit.

Cocaine comes from leaves of the coca plant, which is grown primarily in South America. It can be further refined into crack, which is sold in small doses cheaply on the street, and when smoked provides a very fast high. Crack addicts are often the most desperate of all drug users. Babies born to crack or cocaine addicted mothers often have multiple, and perhaps permanent, problems.

Amphetamines are synthetic stimulants known as "speed." They inspire tremendous energy; users may stay awake for days at a time. Depression and even psychosis follows. These drugs are very debilitating and cause bizarre behaviour.

"Ecstasy", or MDMA, produces euphoria and loving feelings for others. It's the drug of choice at "raves" – huge, all-night music and dance gatherings of young people. Sniffing glue and solvents is a particularly unhealthy addiction. It produces a high but can also stop the heart. LSD is a synthetic drug that induces hallucinations and thought disorders.

None of these drugs are easy to buy, unless you happen to know the right people. People who mistakenly hand money to an undercover narcotics agent can spend a long time in prison.

Just Say No

Every elected or appointed official is conscious of the monumental drug problem in America. The cure is elusive. Many drug addicts are locked up, often for long terms because of mandatory sentencing, and the prison business is a growth industry. There are not nearly enough places in drug rehabilitation programs for the people who want them. Federal attempts to intercept drugs before they reach the street have been so unsuccessful that the current price of heroin on the street has remained stably low for years.

Despite the availability of drugs in schools, you should not worry excessively that your children will fall in with bad friends and start taking drugs. Although it's possible, if they are mature and well directed, they are most unlikely to become steady users.

Alcohol

The most used drug is the legal one – alcohol. The first settlers were very heavy drinkers, and this has long been a hard-drinking country. Recently the consumption of alcohol has dropped, but alcohol still (it is estimated) contributes to over half the crimes committed and most certainly creates a great deal of unhappiness. Many families have at least one member who drinks too much, complete with neglected children and lost jobs.

Alcoholics rarely stop drinking without help, which is available through Alcoholics Anonymous (AA), a worldwide group of sober alcoholics who give up drinking and stay sober by meeting together and helping each other. A listing for AA can be found in nearly every phone book in the country. There are also many treatment programs for alcoholics.

Americans once considered drunk driving inevitable, but attitudes have changed. Drunk driving laws have become quite strict; in many states you automatically lose your license if convicted. If you cause harm, you could go to jail for a long period of time.

If you are stopped by the police and accused of driving "under the influence," you must take the sobriety test offered, or you will be auto-matically convicted. The test will be of your breath, blood, or urine.

MEDICAL CARE

Unlike all other developed countries, there is no national health plan in the USA, and the cost of medical care is staggering. Consequently, you must have private medical insurance. Insurance is costly, but without it illness could ruin you financially. A bed in a New York City hospital can cost $1,900 a day.

In fact, if you don't have insurance, you could be refused admission to a hospital (unless your situation is life-threatening in which case the nearest hospital has to take you) and be forced to go to the overcrowded public hospital – where you will still have to pay, unless you have no money whatsoever.

The medical profession charges up and down the line for each separate service – for X-rays, tests, medicines, and office visits; in

111

addition to your hospital bill you may owe money to surgeons, anaesthesiologists, private nurses, respiratory therapists, pharmacists, and people you scarcely realised existed. You will discover a separate charge for each time your doctor popped into your room and nodded his or her head.

Health Maintenance Organizations (HMOs) are the big trend in healthcare now. In an HMO, you pay a monthly membership and receive whatever services you need at little or no additional cost, but you must use only the services covered by the HMO. Consequently, the HMO, which is usually a profitable corporation, has a strong interest in limiting the amount of treatment you get. If the company decides you truly need a certain treatment, you will get it, but the HMO does the deciding – not you.

Getting Insurance

If you are working for a company here, your employer is likely to at least partially pay for your health insurance, but note that policies rarely cover all medical expenses. If you don't have employee insurance, you will have to find a private plan, and your insurance agent should be able to advise you on short-term insurance. Colleges have health plans for students.

The poor aren't completely without resources. Medicare, a national plan, provides coverage for the old and disabled – but doesn't pay for medication; Medicaid and various state plans cover the indigent. Still, 42 million Americans have no health insurance at all. Most of them work in jobs too marginal to provide medical insurance.

Quality of Care

At its best, American medical care is excellent, and people come from all over the world to have esoteric operations and advanced cancer treatment. In most hospitals your care will be more than adequate, although nurses are extremely busy and rarely linger by your bedside.

As in most countries, it's helpful to have family or friends around to assist with your more mundane needs. However, you will find American hospital wards very quiet. The presumption here is that the sick person needs to rest and to rest he or she has to be alone. So large gatherings at the bedside are rare. Friends arrive with flowers, but make their visits very brief. An alternative to visiting is to send a get-well card or to have a florist make up and deliver a bouquet of flowers to the hospital.

You may find that for a simple ailment you are offered much more extensive and high-technology care than you would get in your own country. This is partly because doctors get sued if they don't consider every possible permutation of a problem. You can refuse treatment that you don't want; if some test or treatment seems extreme, talk over the alternatives with the doctor.

Up-to-date American doctors are encouraged not to be too bossy or domineering and are supposed to be happy to discuss your problems at length – it's considered desirable for patients to understand what is happening to them. Because the doctor shortage is over, patients can afford to walk away from a doctor who is curt or rude.

Very few doctors make house calls; no matter how sick you are you will be expected to appear in their offices unless you are in the hospital. A recognised problem is that in this world of specialists there may be nobody who is in charge of your case. The latest specialty is that of "family medicine" – the doctor who coordinates the specialists.

It's a good idea to line up a doctor – if not a "family" specialist, perhaps an internist – as soon as you arrive if you're staying for an extended period. If anything bad happens, you will need a doctor to admit you to a hospital. Furthermore, most effective drugs, antibiotics for instance, must be prescribed by doctors. So there's a good chance you'll be wanting a doctor sooner or later. If you cannot get recommendations from friends, local medical societies will be glad to give you names.

Mainstream Alternatives

A segment of the population has become increasingly sceptical about modern medicine, which often seems to have lost touch with human and spiritual forces. Occasionally the treatment is worse than the disease, and the reluctance on the part of both doctors and patients to let nature take its course leads to an over-medicated population.

In reaction, people have both started looking after themselves (through diet, exercise, etc.) and have turned to "alternative" health practitioners: acupuncturists, homeopaths, chiropractors (who do not consider themselves "alternative"), nutritionists, Chinese herbalists, and other healers. Time-honoured native remedies are much in vogue among New Age types. Most of the aforementioned healers have the advantage of being at least fairly harmless. But do not assume that because they operate legally there is reason to believe that their cures work. It's strictly *caveat emptor* (Latin for "let the buyer beware") in this department – which admittedly is the case no matter what kind of doctor is treating you.

AIDS

New treatments have reduced the death rate from AIDS, but the disease remains incurable and tragic. The majority of the sufferers are either homosexual men or drug addicts who have shared needles.

You need not worry about contracting AIDS unless you have sexual relations with someone who carries the virus, you shoot drugs with dirty needles, or you receive infected blood in a blood transfusion. The blood supply is tested for the AIDS virus, but the test is not absolutely definitive so it is best not to have a transfusion unless absolutely necessary.

If you feel you must have sexual relations with someone who could carry the AIDS virus, you should use a latex condom. But condoms can fail. Drug addicts and homosexuals are the likeliest AIDS carriers, but heterosexuals are not exempt. The days of exuberant free love in America are over.

Chastity will also protect the visitor from a few other venereal diseases – herpes, syphilis, gonorrhoea – that would be unpleasant to take home.

Do not take up with prostitutes – male or female. Other than in a few counties in the state of Nevada, prostitution is illegal in the USA. Consequently, prostitutes are not subject to disease checks, and many are drug addicts. Furthermore, you could end up being beaten and robbed. The sexual underworld is a dangerous place.

Suing

The practice of dragging one's neighbour, doctor, spouse, host, and employer into court causes shock among newcomers to this country. We are a most litigious people, and we prefer to believe that there is always a responsible party for every event in life.

People have sued for: injuries attained while breaking into houses, losing a spelling bee, being fired, loss of pleasure when injured, emotional distress, tripping on sidewalks, and choking in restaurants. The list of seemingly ridiculous suits provides great mirth and sometimes large awards.

To some degree, the pattern of suing has led to safer places and practices, but to a greater extent it has created high insurance rates and the sacrifice of services. Towns have gone bankrupt when held responsible for accidents on public property. Schools have lost play yards because they can't afford liability insurance. Some churches won't shelter the homeless because they lack the necessary insurance.

Bad as the situation is, some foreigners have picked up an exaggerated idea of it. It is not true that no doctor will ever stop if there's an accident. In many states, a "good Samaritan" law forbids suing a doctor under such circumstances. Families still take friends' children camping . Usually if your friend falls off your garden wall and plans to sue you, he will find out what your insurance is first and the suit can be worked out amicably without much damage to you.

Nonetheless, if someone could break a leg falling through the hole on your front porch, fix it.

Should you decide to do a little suing yourself, bear in mind that it's one thing to sue and win, another to collect. It's not worth the bother of going to court unless you have a realistic chance of seeing the money. Much of the proceeds of a case often end up in the lawyers' hands. Cases drag on for years, and your time will be unpleasantly spent. The two parties to the dispute usually, in one way or another, both lose.

Homelessness

Most immigrants no longer arrive thinking the streets of America will be paved with gold, but neither do they expect to find people sleeping in the streets. This is still the world's richest country. But people live on the streets, by the hundreds, in all the major cities. Thousands more spend nights in temporary shelters, not knowing where they're going to spend the following nights.

America has a housing problem. In the last 35 years, little low-cost housing has been built, and rents and house prices have climbed dizzyingly. What used to be cheap housing is now expensive. It is a much greater struggle than it used to be for a reasonably successful family to afford a house; for marginal people it becomes impossible.

A proportion of the people living on the streets are beyond helping themselves. But an increasing number of the homeless are families or single mothers with children. Some of these have just had a run of bad luck, and others have problems exacerbated by drugs, alcohol, or mental instability. Clearly, the looseness of family ties is a factor – otherwise more of those down on their luck would have a relative to stay with. There are teenagers living on the streets because they have run away or been kicked out of an abusive home.

Foreigners find the homeless situation difficult to comprehend because often in their own countries – no matter how poor – everybody still has a place to stay even if shared with many others. Here, both city governments and private charities try to provide shelters for the homeless, but there is never enough money. The homeless situation is a shameful one for America.

Chapter Seven

GOD AND COUNTRY

Motherhood, God, and the Flag. Any United States politician who hopes to be re-elected must take these three sacred icons seriously. While most foreigners will easily comprehend the tributes paid to motherhood, the attitude to religion remains confusing to many and that towards the flag mystifying.

In God We Trust

The American viewpoint on religion is paradoxical. We honour the separation of Church and State (and the freedom to worship in the religion of one's choice), but in public life few people dare admit to having no religious belief at all.

The Supreme Court keeps watch over freedom of religion – prayer is not allowed in schools or during public sports events. Religion is supposed to be a private matter, between the individual, his conscience, and his Church.

Nonetheless, there is a widespread feeling that decent people believe in God and that ethical standards spring from religion. Politicians frequently assure the electorate of their faith in God. The President says in his State of the Union address, "God is near," and the White House holds regular prayer breakfasts.

Our coins all have "In God We Trust" cast on them; the Pledge of Allegiance to the Flag calls us "one nation, under God." Presumably, some of this religiosity is left over from the early founders.

Religious cults have been prominent through our history. Religious belief jibes with American optimism and the faith that justice will prevail, if not in this world, then in the next.

Despite thriving churches, the US is a very secular society – in the minds of some visitors, too secular. They see a country in moral decline, where people have so much personal freedom that society is in chaos.

Nobody could deny that a great deal of what meets the eye – billboards, television, magazines – is vulgar. However, people should not imagine that American's lives are truly reflected on the advertising space.

The Christian Majority

It's the Christian God that most people have in mind when they invoke Him. In the United States, 86% of the population describe themselves as Christians; 2% are Jewish; Muslims and Buddhists are 0.5% each. About 13% claim no religion, and the rest are divided between thousands of other religions, old and new. The only national religious holidays are Christian holidays. However, employers must respect the demands of anyone's religion and grant leave of absence when religion requires it.

Photo: Esther Wanning

Parishioners linger to chat after church on Sunday morning. With the idea of showing respect in "God's house," people usually dress up to go to church.

Nine out of ten Americans claim to believe in God, and one-half are affiliated with a religious group. However, foreigners shouldn't imagine that the average American is deeply involved with his religion (although some are). We only expect our leaders to have some faith in God, not to take their religion more seriously than their golf games.

Sectarianism

A majority (52%) of Americans are Protestants – Christians who do not follow the Church of Rome (Catholicism). As Protestants have no central authority, there are hundreds of denominations. All adhere to one God and the Bible, differently interpreted. Some have very dignified services, whereas others involve a lot of emotional display. As a general rule, it's the dignified ones (Episcopalian, Congregational, Presbyterian) that are the more upper class, and many a rising salesman has switched from the Baptist to the Episcopalian Church when he moved to a better neighbourhood.

Most of the remaining Christians are Catholics (24%), a group by and large reflecting Irish, Italian, and South American immigrants. The Catholics have known discrimination and even (unjustifiably) have been suspected of dividing their allegiances between the Roman Pope and their country. Until the election of John F. Kennedy, people thought that no Catholic could become president.

The only other Christian group of any size are the Mormons, which comprise 2% of the population. Besides these established religions, there are numerous religious cults. Most cults depend on a charismatic leader and usually don't outlast him or her. Cults demand a wholehearted commitment from the followers, and scandals erupt among them frequently.

Various Hindu and Buddhist leaders have attracted a significant following in recent years. Some of these leaders are learned messengers from the East, and others acquire power and wealth, while making a little learning go a long way.

121

"Born Agains"

The "Born Again Christians" are the most surprising among today's religious sects. Not long ago, intellectuals assumed that in the modern scientific age, belief in God would not last much longer. They were wrong. Instead, millions of people have joined a variety of fundamentalist groups. These people, who include President George W. Bush, are collectively called "Born Agains", because they believe that their lives started anew when they accepted Jesus Christ into their lives. They hold the Bible, despite its contradictions, to be literally true – which leads to the problem of evolution.

Darwin or Adam?

The Bible says that God made the world and the first man and woman (Adam and Eve) in six days. (On the seventh, he rested, which is why Sunday is supposed to be a day of rest among Christians.) If this is true, the theory of evolution, as described by Charles Darwin, must be wrong. So say the fundamentalists. The evolutionists say that man evolved over millions of years.

The evidence is strongly on the side of Darwin, but for the sake of those who cling to the Bible's teachings, some states have actually compelled teachers to teach both sides. Over this issue, many fundamentalists have withdrawn their children from public schools altogether and enrolled them in Christian schools.

The fundamentalists are usually not highly educated and are strongest in the South. Their rise may come from the desire, amid the confusion of modern life, to return to a simpler society. Fundamentalist preachers can be seen on many cable television stations, and visitors should try to watch them at least once. However, they should not mistake these preachers as representing mainstream thinking.

Abortion

The other big issue that brings out religious divisions is abortion. Presently, in most states, any woman who so desires may have an

Photo: The Weekly Packet

This man, bowing his head in prayer at the annual Blessing of the Fleet in a coastal town in Maine, is prompting his dog to bow its head in prayer too.

abortion, but there is a strong movement (called "Right to Life") to make abortion illegal. The campaign against abortion is rooted in the religious belief that all human life is sacred and begins at conception, but many feminists think that the real root is the desire to keep women subservient and pregnant.

The Catholic Church considers contraception as well as abortion immoral. However, Catholic women actually practice birth control as much as other American women do.

123

Charities

Judeo-Christian values emphasize the importance of aiding the poor and unfortunate. Many of the hungry are fed from church basements, and some of the country's largest charities are run by a church group. Hospitals, homeless shelters, workshops for the disabled, schools, teen centers, and countless other projects are church or synagogue-supported – although often run without any overt religious overtones.

Churches also often support missionaries who go to distant lands to spread the Gospel. Many of them also work as teachers or doctors.

The Flag

Patriotism comes close to being a religion in America. Patriots demonstrate their love of America and freedom through respect for the flag. Politicians make a lot of noise over loving the flag and the country. It is nearly impossible for a politician to look realistically at America's problems because he or she might appear not to believe that the USA is and always will be the greatest country in the world.

Citizens of other countries pay homage to their flags too, but the belligerence with which Americans proclaim their patriotism is surprising to outsiders. In many countries, to insist that your country is the best country of all is unpleasantly chauvinistic. But Americanism means believing America is a special nation chosen by God.

Professional sports events begin with the singing of the national anthem (whereupon men take their hats off and some people put their hands on their hearts). The flag waves above all government offices. Although the Supreme Court has ruled that the right to burn the flag is protected, there are still laws (mostly unenforced) about bringing the flag in after dark, not wearing it, and not trampling upon it.

Many schools begin each day with the students standing up and facing the flag with their hands on their hearts, saying "I pledge allegiance to the flag of the United States of America and to the Republic for which it stands – one nation, under God, indivisible, with liberty and justice for all."

Chapter Eight

EDUCATION

It is largely by passing through our public school system that immigrant families from all over the world have come to identify themselves as thoroughly American, registering American values, culture, and folklore. Without this educational filter, it's doubtful if the American experiment could have worked.

American public schools provide free schooling to every child from ages 5 to 18 – or from kindergarten through 12th grade. Because each of the fifty states runs its own schools, school requirements vary across the nation, and there is no federal testing of students. In most states, attendance is mandatory until age 16. Where and when the school system works, it provides the means for someone from the poorest home to advance in society.

The Educational Prescription

The object of the American school system is to bestow a broad education on every youngster. This is not an overly ambitious goal. Only a few students are expected to become intellectuals or scholars. The rest, we hope, will be able to read, write, think, and deal with the issues of the day. In keeping with the democratic principle, there are no absolute turning points, such as when a crucial exam separates the sheep from the goats. Theoretically, anyone who completes high school is college material.

Problems

Currently, our schools are a source of intense distress because many of our younger citizens, despite 13 continuous years' of school attendance, are profoundly ignorant. Few know where Alaska is, what the Bill of Rights is, when World War II was fought, or who Thomas Jefferson was. One of my friends, the principal of an exclusive private school, discovered to his chagrin that not one of his 8th graders had any idea what the circumference of the world might be.

In math and science tests comparing American youngsters with those of other nations, Americans do fairly well in elementary grades, but their performances worsen in higher grades. Still, the top 10 percent of American students, while short on facts, are probably as able and skilled as the best students anywhere. But the bottom 50 percent are barely literate and struggle with basic math. Whether this is solely the fault of the schools or whether families and communities are equally to blame is the subject of great debate.

Concern about the educational system is nearly always couched in terms of national needs. If the next generation can't read, who will run the businesses? If they can't compute, how will we compete with the rest of the world?

Education for its own sake, for the sheer love of knowledge, does not get much press.

For many students, school is a happy experience. But it can also be anguishing. Overall, public schools are not nurturing places, and the competition for grades is minor compared to the competition for being "cool", wearing the right clothes, and having the right friends. The harassment of anyone a little peculiar, unathletic or unpopular can be serious. Because schools are often so large and the cast of characters changes constantly, it is very easy for a child to feel lost and friendless. In 1999, at Columbine High School in Colorado, two alienated students carried out a massacre, killing thirteen people and themselves and wounding many more. Whatever their reasons, it cannot be coincidental that Columbine High is a large (2,000 students), White, suburban school, where athletic prowess far outranks academic brilliance.

Schools have various cliques – jocks, brains, nerds, Goths – but there isn't a place for everyone. However, many of those who suffer miserably through high school find grown-up life rich and rewarding, while for some popular high school jocks, life afterwards is never as bright again.

Educational Philosophy

For the past sixty years our schools have operated on the theories of John Dewey (1859–1952), an American educator and writer. Dewey believed that the school's job was to enhance the natural development of the growing child, rather than to pour information, for which the child had no context, into him or her. In the Dewey system, the child becomes the active agent in his own education, rather than a passive receptacle for facts.

Consequently, American schools are very enthusiastic about teaching "life skills" – logical thinking, analysis, creative problem solving. The actual content of the lessons is secondary to the process, which is supposed to train the child to be able to handle whatever life may present, including all the unknowns of the future. Students and teachers both regard pure memorisation as uncreative and somewhat vulgar.

In addition to "life skills," schools are assigned to solve the ever growing stock of social problems. Racism, teenage pregnancy, alcoholism, drug use, reckless driving, and suicide are just a few of the modern problems that have appeared on the school curriculum. All this contributes to a high degree of social awareness in American youngsters.

School Structure

At the age of five, children start kindergarten, where they concentrate on getting ready for the heavier burdens of elementary school by singing songs, painting pictures, learning to hang up their coats, and identifying numbers and letters. Grades 1 through 5 or 6 are known as elementary or grade school, and at the very least teach reading, writing, and arithmetic, along with varying degrees of art, music, gym (sports), social studies, and science. The curriculum usually broadens in middle school or junior high (which can be anything from 5th to 8th grade to just 7th and 8th grade), and by high school (which traditionally begins with 9th grade) a wide choice of elective courses may be offered – including such unacademic subjects as car repair, typing, homemaking, and art.

Those in their first year of high school, 9th grade, are called freshmen; 10th graders are sophomores; 11th graders are juniors; and 12th graders are seniors. (This terminology repeats itself in college when first-year students are freshmen, second-year students are sophomores, and so on.)

Student Life

To the students, the most notable difference between elementary school and the higher levels is that in junior high they start "changing classes." This means that rather than spending the day in one class-

Cub scouts at a Memorial Day parade. Cub scouts and the older boy scouts take an oath to be "trustworthy, loyal, helpful, friendly, courteous, kind, obedient, cheerful, thrifty, brave, clean, and reverent."

room, they switch classrooms to meet their different teachers. This gives them three or four minutes between classes in the hallways, where a great deal of the important social action of high school traditionally takes place. Students have lockers in these hallways, around which they congregate.

Society in general does not take the business of studying very seriously. Once foreign children have learned English, they may find their studies ridiculously easy and be bored. Schoolchildren have a great deal of free time, which they are encouraged to fill with extracurricular activities – sports, clubs, cheerleading, scouts – supposed to inculcate such qualities as leadership, sportsmanship, ability to organise things, etc. Those who don't become engaged in such activities or have after-school jobs have plenty of opportunity to "hang out", listen to teenage music, and watch television.

Compared to other nations, American students do not have much homework. Studies also show that American parents have lower expectations for their children's success in school than other nationalities do. (Historically, there has not been much correlation between American school success and success in later life.) "He's just not a scholar," the American parents might say, content that their son is on the swim team and doesn't take drugs. (Some of the young do choose to study hard, for reasons of their own, such as determining that the road to riches lies through Harvard Business School.)

What American schools do effectively teach is the competitive method. In innumerable ways children are pitted against each other whether in classroom discussion, spelling bees, reading groups, or tests. Every classroom is expected to produce a scattering of A's and F's (A = excellent; B = good; C = average; D = poor; and F = failed). A teacher who gives all A's looks too soft – so students are aware that they are competing for the limited number of top marks.

Foreign students sometimes don't understand that copying from other people's papers or from books is considered wrong and taken seriously. Here, it is important to show that you have done your own work and are displaying your own knowledge. It is more important than helping your friends to pass, whom we think do not deserve to pass unless they can provide their own answers. Group effort goes against the competitive grain, and American students do not study together as many Asians do. Many Asians in this country consider their group study habits a large contributor to their school success.

The Ever-Blowing Winds of Change

Sadly, the current school situation caps 40 years of well-intentioned reform. The progressivism of the Sixties was successful in making school curriculums more sensitive to the cultures of students not belonging to the White, Christian majority. Most of the old textbooks were thrown out for being too sexist and ethnocentric and were replaced by textbooks that attempted to tell the stories of every minority group. There was a massive and largely unsuccessful attempt to integrate the school system so that Black, Hispanic and Asian students would have equal opportunity to attend better schools. The term "busing" referred to the practice of transporting students by bus out of their neighbourhoods to a school lacking in minority students.

Unfortunately, one response to busing was for many White people to move to suburban towns, or to send their children to private schools. Today, many urban schools don't have very many White students left to add to the racial mix.

The ideals of the 1960s also included a thrust towards "relevance in education" – even more lively exploration by the students, even less memorisation. A great democratisation blew through the schools, and the subject of students' rights was taken very seriously. Dress codes were thrown out, required subjects became few, a teacher's word was no longer law. If students could be themselves and pursue their own interests, went the thinking, then they'd get a real education.

The wind is blowing the other way now. Admirable as the ideology sounded, the fruit has not been a crop of inspired, self-motivated students. Instead, test scores sank, disrespect for teachers fell to a new low, discipline became the number one problem in many schools, and students' own interests led more often in the direction of drugs than towards intellectual endeavour.

The current hope is that new state standardised tests will provide the means to force failing schools to toe the mark. Early results do seem to be positive. However, teachers argue that such tests make the curriculum more boring than ever and detract from real learning.

Teacher Respect

Teaching is not a high-status occupation in the United States. This is in keeping with the pay scale, which is low compared to other professions. (In another country, one could be respected and poor, but rarely in America.) Furthermore, teaching has traditionally been a woman's field, another strike against it. And in all truth, many teachers are not well-educated, having frequently been trained in teaching methods rather than in an academic field.

Teachers are treated poorly inside as well as outside the schools. They are seen as the foot soldiers who must carry out the constant flow of orders descending from school boards, politicians, principals, and parents. Every year, in the worst schools, teachers are injured by students. Students' rights remain paramount, and teachers must be prepared to justify their actions in all matters.

Many foreigners have rather simplistically concluded that it's the absence of corporal punishment (which is illegal in many states) in the schools that causes all the problems, but few Americans would agree. To Americans, corporal punishment is unfair, giving too much power to the strong.

Some school systems have begun to have students wear uniforms. Contrary as uniforms are to traditional American freedom of expression, these schools hope uniforms will have a calming effect. The need to wear the right clothes creates a lot of social pressure in schools, and where gangs are strong, just wearing the wrong colours can be dangerous. What's more, the sexiness of current teen girls' clothing cannot help be distracting to teenaged boys. However, where uniforms are required, the courts hold that students be allowed to opt out of wearing them on religious or free-speech grounds.

School Choices

Not every school is a jungle. There are also sterling schools free of danger or of discipline problems of note and from which students get top grades in nationwide exams. High schools offer a very wide variety of courses and separate the college-bound students from the vocational ones. In many schools, even when the average standard is low, an excellent education is available to those who take advantage. "You could learn an awful lot here if you listened," said a visiting Swedish student of her suburban high school.

However, if you are packing your child off to the local school, you cannot assume that it will be satisfactory. You must investigate, preferably before deciding where to live. Many Americans consider a good local school one of the most important criteria in choosing a neighbourhood.

Better schools are generally in better areas, but there are scattered success stones everywhere. Poor neighbourhoods in big cities may have so-called "magnet" schools, which emphasise particular studies and attract students from all over the city. Some large cities also have at least one select high school, which requires high grades and test scores for admission. These schools are as high-pressure and prestigious as any private school.

By law, schools must provide an education for all students, even those who cannot function in an ordinary classroom. Consequently there are numerous "special" programs for handicapped, troubled, and "developmentally disabled" (retarded) children.

Beating the System

Overall, unless you're living in a small, one-school town, the school set-up is complicated. Your address determines your child's school assignment, but often it is possible to change that assignment. Perhaps the only way to learn the ins and outs of your local school system is to talk to other parents. You will probably not find it written down anywhere that School A is a good school and School B a bad one. Or School C may be very good if you can get into the gifted program (a fast-track program) and otherwise you're better off elsewhere. These are the things you'll find out by gossiping in the local laundromat.

You may also discover that you have a good chance of getting into School E if you come from a certain ethnic group, or that if you are really keen on entering School D, you must line up very early in the morning on a certain day.

Or Escaping

You may instead decide to follow many Americans (of all colours) to the suburbs. Nice suburbs have fairly safe, homogeneous schools. Another alternative, one chosen by one in eleven American children, is a private school. (Private schools are ones to which parents pay tuition; public schools are supported by taxes.)

Gaining entrance to the well-known schools is highly competitive. In large cities, there are private schools for every need – from the intellectually advanced to the learning disabled. There are also religious schools and schools adhering to particular educational philosophies. But bear in mind that there are affluent city-dwellers who send their children to public schools merely because they want their children to have the broader social experience of a public school.

Lastly, there are boarding schools, mostly for 9th through 12th grades. Some of the old New England boarding schools have educated generations of families. Happily, in recent years these "snob" schools have made considerable efforts to recruit students from varied backgrounds. Simply being a foreigner may make your child a desirable candidate from the school's point of view.

Private school costs might run from $3,600 a year for a religious school (and you don't have to be a Catholic to go to a Catholic school) to $21,000 a year for an exclusive school. Nearly all private schools have some scholarships, and the oldest ones have endowments large enough for them to accept anyone they want – regardless of ability to pay the high tuition fees.

Universities

Over half of high school graduates go on to some kind of advanced study so there is nothing exclusive about a college education. At last count, there were more than 3,000 institutions of higher learning in the United States. This includes everything from two-year colleges with a few hundred students to state universities (a university offers both a four-year undergraduate program and advanced degrees from its various graduate schools) with 35,000 students on one campus.

Nearly every college charges tuition. State universities are much cheaper than private ones, where total costs including room and board can be as much as $35,000 a year, not including books. While this sounds staggering, at many colleges as many as two-thirds of the students are receiving scholarships.

Despite the plethora of colleges, every year tension mounts as high school seniors wait to find out if the colleges of their choice have accepted them. The criteria for acceptance include high school grades, personal recommendations, achievements outside school, and test scores. These tests consist of nationwide, though private, exams known as SAT's (Scholastic Aptitude Tests), which test both mathematics and verbal skills, and Achievement Tests, which test knowledge in particular subjects. Although important, these tests do not inspire any of the suicidal impulses that university exams in some other countries do.

A status education is available only from the relatively few high-profile institutions among the many, although an excellent education is actually available at most schools. It is conversely possible to go to one of the "best" schools and emerge with a dim education. The standards for completing the course may not be as demanding as those for entrance, and students often find they have a great deal of time to "party." Some schools are best known for such qualities as the regular drunkenness of their students or the excellent nearby skiing. Sports

135

teams, especially the football team, may be a college's greatest claim to fame. Colleges recruit players with potential to become professional athletes, and not based on academic skills. The football coach is likely to be the highest paid person on campus, and millions are spent on maintaining sports programs. The hope is that successful teams will produce alumnae who donate generously.

Despite the frequently immature pursuits of the students, in the last thirty years universities have relinquished their parental role. Most colleges do very little to regulate the lives of students, other than to dismiss those who fail too many courses and to offer counseling to the troubled. Teachers do not involve themselves in the lives of their students. Parents who want supervision for their young might have to find a Christian college.

A Tanzanian who arrived here to attend Corning Community College says he'll never forget the first day's registration: "It was terrible, overwhelming. I had never had to choose my courses before. This would never happen in Africa." American colleges require certain basic courses (varying with each college), but beyond these leave students free to pursue their own interests. Consequently, nearly every institution has a fat catalogue with a giant smorgasbord of courses – from social relations among the Inuit to nuclear physics.

Graduate Schools

Beyond the parties, remedial courses, and football teams, there is a higher level at which the American university is manifestly successful. It is in the graduate schools that the American academic system shines, where intelligent inquiry and the analytic tradition pay off.

The serious student who reaches the advanced levels will be as well trained as at any university in the world. Professors from around the world flock to American universities as much for the intellectual excitement as for the handsome salaries. (Professors are held in much higher esteem than school teachers, which is reflected in their salaries as well as in a much greater degree of autonomy in their teaching.) Increasingly, foreigners occupy a large number of places in American graduate schools, particularly in the sciences.

The Classroom

The participatory classroom is the American ideal. Teachers want evidence that the students are interested, listening, and excited. Usually, this comes in the form of questions, and students are sometimes graded on "classroom participation." Foreigners are often surprised that the teacher wants to hear what they think and what they don't understand. Teachers even welcome disagreement.

There is, however, in nearly every class one student who talks too much and bores everybody. You should not become so carried away with the American system that you become this student.

Teachers may want very much for their students to learn, but they do not feel insulted if a student does not understand, or responsible if a student fails. The ultimate effort is up to the student.

The Licensing of America

A century ago, very few occupations required licensing. Doctors, lawyers, and accountants learned their trades through apprenticeships. Today, those who want to go into these reliably lucrative fields need years of postgraduate training. Even many service occupations, such as beautician, electrician, and plumber, have training requirements that restrict membership.

Until World War II, many successful businessmen had little schooling; now most prospective managers need college degrees, and those with an MBA (Master of Business Administration) are most in demand. A degree from one of the prestigious schools commands a high starting salary. Teachers and social workers, besides acquiring a bachelor's degree (conferred on completing the undergraduate course) must submit to specialized training.

137

This is a trend that James Fallows, one of our more alert social observers, deplores. At its best, he explains in his book, *More Like Us,* America was a country with enormous receptivity for anyone who could do the task at hand, regardless of whether or not he had specific credentials. The diploma mill, he is convinced, has done little to improve people's skills. It just serves to keep people in their places – an unhealthy development for this country, keeping people without academic talent or tuition fees from getting ahead. Furthermore, as one only has one youth to spend in preparation, lengthy training greatly restricts people's flexibility. Fallows suggests we change our system to encourage the talented teachers and the gifted doctors, instead of the drones. Until then, he is correct in observing that degrees do matter, and for many fields, it is worth the effort of getting one.

Adult Education

After complaining about many aspects of American life, a 40-year-old woman from Hong Kong concluded, "But where else could someone my age go back to school and get a degree in social work? Here you can change your whole life, start a new business, do what you really want to do."

So at least to this person, school requirements weren't inhibiting. And to millions of others, adult education is the path to a new career, or if not to a new career, to a new outlook. Schools generally encourage the older person who wants to start anew, and besides regular classes, schedule evening classes in special programs. Today there are so many people of retirement age in college that it is no longer remarkable.

Chapter Nine

FRIENDS

There's often a disappointment waiting for the newcomer who takes American friendliness at face value. Americans are indiscriminate with their smiles and their chatter. Foreigners (those who come from places where people don't behave like friends unless they are friends) on arrival may be delighted to find themselves the objects of much enthusiastic attention. They may imagine they may have instantly acquired a bunch of fine friends. "But it doesn't mean anything," says an Indian woman.

"Often the first American we sit down and talk to is at the employment agency, and she's so nice we think we've got this wonderful new friend. Then we find out it was just for profit, and we never hear from her again. We're disillusioned."

This is not to say that Americans will always let you down. Many foreigners have found Americans to be not only friendly, but loyal and helpful. However, the mobility of American life has made the term "friend" less profound than elsewhere.

In many countries, most friends date from school days, and it is hard to make new ones thereafter. For Americans it is the exception rather than the rule to remain in one place, and the school friends (who may have changed every year anyhow) are usually left behind. New friends rise up to fill new stages of life. Even when the locale remains the same, new friends step in to match life changes: college friends, work friends, club friends, neighbours, new-hobby friends, sports friends, friends-with-same-age-children.

Frequently, each friend fills a particular niche. There's the friend with whom I discuss certain problems, the one with whom I play tennis, the one with whom I work. When anything changes – my problems go away, I quit tennis, I get a new job – I may stop seeing those particular friends. If I'm lucky, I will have a few lifelong friends, but these could be scattered about the world.

The Rules

Once I've got a friend, I'll be careful not to presume on him or her. That we might be "bothering" someone is an everlasting concern of Americans, even among good friends.

"Irish people live in each other's pockets," said one woman. "It's completely different here. You keep your distance."

I will be very hesitant to ask friends for favours – one of my attractions as a friend is that I am not demanding. If I were, my prospective friends would be likely to back off. Neediness scares people. Rather than having to refuse a request, we prefer to have friends we can trust to make their requests rare and reasonable.

We ourselves do not wish to be indebted to anybody else. We like reciprocal arrangements because they keep the scales balanced. This week I drive my friend to the airport; next week she drives me. A Chinese woman related that she tried to join a childcare cooperative, but she found the accounting system so complex (to make sure that no one person did more than anyone else) that it drove her crazy.

Eventually in a friendship one can begin to take small services for granted – the loan of a dress, a phone call to find out vital information – but no one expects a real sacrifice. No matter how desperately my friend might need a babysitter, she would never ask me to miss a day's work to take care of her child. I have sometimes been very confused when foreign friends did remarkable things for me – drove me great distances or took the subway to the airport to meet me. Such things are not in our vocabulary, and I find it difficult to respond.

For the average American, the feeling of being indebted is practically a physical pain. We would rather buy an expensive tool we'll hardly ever use than have to borrow one. When a neighbour had to store some things in my freezer (which was no trouble for me) after hers broke down, she could not rest until she had made me a special dinner. I rescued another neighbour's runaway dog, and she bought me a cake. In point of fact, most of us are human and like to be helpful and would not mind receiving only thanks for a good deed.

But even this constant thanking of others perturbs some foreigners. "Why are you always thanking each other?" says a Palestinian. "At home, I expect my friends to help me. If I'm moving, all I have to do is mention when to my friends and they'll all show up. I would never have to say please. Thanks aren't necessary. I show up when they move. People are very selfish here."

Attitudes are different in small towns where people know each other and each other's families well and, besides, don't have the money to buy tools they will use once a year. Here, a great deal of socialising goes on in the name of borrowing and returning things. In the cities, affluence has afforded independence, but it is significant that Americans would rather put their money into independence than into other luxuries.

Best Friends

In the special category of lifelong friends, the favour score card is not so carefully kept. But here the potential for favour-giving must be more or less equal. This is one reason it is difficult to have good friends across economic gaps. If you fly me to your villa in Spain, how can I possibly repay you?

Privacy

"In Malaysia, you don't have to hire a caterer," says one friend of mine. "If we're having a party, our friends all come early to help."

Here, one reason I'm not going to arrive in the morning to help out is that I would be infringing on the party-givers' privacy. They probably don't want to have anyone in their house but family – or hired help – until the first guest arrives, and they don't want me looking inside their cupboards and listening to them bicker about how many bottles of wine to buy.

Furthermore, if I insist on helping, I would seem to be suggesting that they are unable to manage alone. Even when I have a very close friend in need, I will go to lengths to appear not to be inconveniencing myself by helping. Part of my kindness to my friend is to act as if I think she can manage perfectly well without me.

Perhaps she is sick. I will make a casserole dish for her and take it to her house, which is some distance away. I may tell her that the dish was something left over after feeding my family (when in fact I may have shopped and cooked especially to make it for her) and that I happened to be in her area anyhow (highly unlikely). She may suspect the truth but will appreciate my consideration for her feelings.

Big Trouble

All this delicacy is very tough on people who are really in trouble. Middle-class Americans are largely protected against catastrophe, but when big trouble does strike such as a long illness in the family –

it can be disillusioning to discover that one's friends are not going to do very much. The troubled family may be desperate enough to accept any amount of help, but their friends scarcely know how to offer and, besides, are not in the habit of sacrificing much time for others.

A Japanese man told me how terribly isolated he felt when he was going through his divorce here. No support net closed around him as it would have in Japan. American friends wouldn't have wanted to insult him by appearing to think he was needy. Indeed, an American might even feel smothered by too much attention, even though most people would probably appreciate more phone calls than they get.

Some foreigners have observed that Americans prefer to help in an institutionalised way. In the AIDS crisis, many people have volunteered through agencies to help the sick. The sick person feels more comfortable calling the agency than calling his friends; his need is legitimised. The volunteer finds the agency route more straightforward than trying to help a friend who is sick and who would probably endlessly protest, "Oh, please, you've done too much already."

These protests are for the self-esteem of the recipient. You can assume that if someone offers to do something for you, he would genuinely like to do it. Because we don't feel responsible for others, we don't offer anything we don't want to deliver. And if the offer is turned down, we will also take the refusal at face value.

I do not mean to convince readers that they will find no helpful friends. Many people in America do not live by the "rules" outlined here, and the country is full of good souls who exist to be of use to others. For true Christians, giving is supposed to be the heart of their religion, so by all means let them practise it.

Neighbours

It can come as a disappointment to foreigners to move into an American community and discover neighbours whose neighbourliness ends with saying hello. In many countries to be a neighbour presumes a relationship. Here, it can be almost the opposite.

Since early days in America, heterogeneous groups have lived side by side, but living side by side didn't mean they liked each other. When a Scotsman staked out his claim on the frontier, he didn't know who would move in next. It could be a German, a Norwegian, a Jew – someone who wasn't his kind. It was true that people needed each other out in the wild, but they were also suspicious of each other.

We remain cautious in approaching our neighbours until we find out what kind of people they are. The neighbour is in a position to be the biggest bother of anyone we know. This is the person who could drop in any time, comment on our comings and goings, do weird things with our children. One might retort that this is also the person who could most conveniently be helpful to us, but help we're not supposed to need.

One reason people move from small towns to big cities is to get away from nosey neighbours, to live in anonymity. The price, of course, is isolation.

Homogeneous communities are closer. On military compounds or in university housing you will find groups who reach out readily to the new arrivals in their midst. A factor separating neighbours is that even the inhabitants on a block of identically priced houses may have little in common. A blue-collar worker who spends all weekend watching sports on television may live next door to a poet who spends her spare time weaving. On the other side, you may have computer programmers living in another world entirely.

The design of houses and the privacy of garages also limit neighbourliness. It is possible to live next door to someone and simply never meet him. In the suburbs, whereas people used to pause to chat when they arrived home in the evening, now the automatic garage door opener allows them to glide into their garages and disappear with only a wave. Gardens bring neighbours together, but in the long summer evenings people are more likely to be indoors watching television than working the earth.

As might be expected, there are many lonely people in America. A Brazilian told me that she thinks people watch television so much because they have no neighbours to talk to. An Arab immigrant finds life very empty here: "I just go to work and come home and eat dinner and go to bed. Life here is just for making money. My soul aches."

Moving On

Some neighbors do become fast friends, and you shouldn't assume that you won't. What is likely, though, is that you or your neighbours are going to be moving on at some point, and you will have to start all over again making friends with somebody else. Nearly one out of five Americans moves every year.

A person's feeling of community often does not come from the place he lives. Some people's community is the workplace, or their community is made up of a group of people with similar interests. People may spend their spare time communicating with strangers on the internet, and even consider them some sort of a community. Household isolation is exacerbated by the increasingly great distances people live from their work, and the time they spend commuting leaves that much less time for community activities.

Meeting and Greeting

INTRODUCTIONS: Introductions are casual here and do not signify much (unlike countries where an introduction establishes a relationship). It is more polite to introduce two people than not to, and it places neither under an obligation. If you are with one friend and encounter another, you need only say, "Ralph Scott, this is Mike Phan."

The more honoured party is the one introduced to (in this case, Ralph), but this quaint rule needn't concern you much. Status is of little matter here. Unless there is business at hand, nobody need produce a card (and often not then). When introduced, you only respond with a smile and "Nice to meet you" or "How are you?" (To which the reply is, "Fine, thank you.") If you are seated and the other person is standing, you should rise, unless you are a lady to whom a man is being introduced. Conversation may or may not ensue.

HANDSHAKES: People meeting for business and older people greeting each other socially usually shake hands. People who see each other regularly would not ordinarily shake hands. Men shake hands more than women. If two couples are introduced at a party, the men would shake hands and the women may or may not. Shaking hands adds an extra cordiality. Shaking hands on leaving a party is entirely optional. No one will think you rude if you don't, but anybody is glad to shake any hand that is offered.

Do grip the other person's hand firmly (but not so firmly as to crush the bones) and give a couple of springy pumps up and down. The passive extending of a hand, leaving someone else to do the work of shaking, leaves a bad impression. People will think you're either conceited or lazy.

Photo: Kristy MacDonald

A firm grip, a smile, and a direct gaze into the other person's eyes make up a proper handshake.

THE SOCIAL KISS: One form of greeting widely replaces the handshake – the pseudo-kiss. To execute this, one leans forward from the waist and presses one's cheek against the other person's, simultaneously kissing the air. One hand usually comes up to simulate a hug, except the hand will stop short of the back and grab the shoulder. While appearing to add warmth, this hand may actually be protecting against too much body contact. Or the hand may pat the other person's back, which is an assertion that what is going on has no sexual meaning. The two people will avoid pressing their bodies together. You go through this routine on one cheek only.

This kind of kissing is routine among sophisticates and even business acquaintances. It means little. Women and women do it; men and women do it. Men and men do not do it; they stick to handshakes.

MEN STUFF: Back-slapping is acceptable among men. So is a touch or a squeeze of the shoulder. But only ball players in their moments of triumph are certifiably masculine enough to throw their arms around each other.

The New Sensitive Male cropped up in the 1970s in reaction to the too-macho standoffish man of the last generation. This new breed does a lot of self-conscious hugging, but most men limit bodily same-sex contact to throwing an arm around another's shoulders.

Couples In Love

Public displays of affection between couples, disgusting to some Asians, are acceptable here. Deep soulful kissing in broad daylight is not in good taste, but we would not consider it shocking either. Handholding, touching, squeezing, and even little kisses are to us just couples properly demonstrating their mutual happiness. Only if a couple is too wrapped up in each other to notice the others present would we consider it rude and make jokes about it later.

When teenagers "can't keep their hands off each other," their parents may not be charmed, but they find some compensation in noting their children's normal sexual adjustment.

Photos: Kristy MacDonald

This sequence shows the social kiss as two women greet each other. Note that despite the obvious warmth, the bodily contact is actually quite limited. The kiss itself flies off into the air.

Photo: The Weekly Packet

A high school baseball team celebrating its victory. Sports victories provide acceptable occasions for boys or men to hug each other.

Friend or Boyfriend?

Women usually have women friends while men have men friends, but it is perfectly possible for friendships to cross gender lines. Women like to feel that a man's interest in them needn't be sexual. But partly because there is often some confusion about whether it is or isn't, close male-female friendships are in the minority.

Foreign men need to realise that the seeming looseness of American women (or girls) does not mean that they are sexually available. Although many young unmarried American women are not virgins, many have no desire to go to bed with someone they do not love, and few wish to have sex with many men.

In some countries, if a woman makes friendly overtures it means she's offering sex. Here, it emphatically does not. A woman may act especially nice because she feels sorry for a poor man alone in a foreign country. When the man misconstrues her kindness as a desire for sex, she is infuriated.

149

The same is true of skimpily dressed women. Skintight jeans, see-through tops, and bikini bathing suits may clothe a girl who hopes to catch a man's eye, but her style of dress should not be taken to indicate that any man will do or that she combines sex and the profit motive.

What Do I Call You?

It was not so thirty years ago, but first names are now the rule in America. If Ralph meets Mike through Dan, all will immediately call each other by first names. Socially, only in the most formal circles, or when a young person is addressing someone considerably older, need one hesitate before risking the first name.

The first name is the given name. Most babies also get a middle name, which is less used. The last name is the family name and is inherited from the father. Thirty years ago, women universally took their husbands' family names upon marriage, sometimes keeping their former last name as a middle name. A woman might then become Harriet Beecher (her father's name) Stowe (her husband's name). She would be known widely as Mrs. (which denotes a married woman) Stowe, and letters would arrive addressed to Mrs. Calvin Stowe. Her husband would remain forever Mr. Calvin Stowe.

Times have changed, and the women's movement has made many women reluctant to change their names for the sake of a husband. Thus Catherine Zeta-Jones does not become Catherine Douglas when she marries Michael Douglas. She might occasionally be called Mrs. Douglas but could not properly be called Mrs. Zeta-Jones because that would make her the Mrs. of someone named Zeta-Jones, which she is not.

That leaves her with two possible titles: Miss Zeta-Jones, which is the usual title for an unmarried woman or girl but is proper for married women retaining their own last names, or else Ms. Zeta-Jones – pronounced mizz – which is the feminist alternative to Mr. and does not denote a marital state. Ms. is widely used in newspapers and on business letters but is less often spoken.

These complications and the fact that so many women have divorced and remarried makes it much easier just to call everyone by first name. This only leaves the problem that using a first name connotes a familiarity that not everybody likes. An older person, in particular, may much prefer that people with whom she does business call her Mrs. Stevens rather than Mary.

Your friend's friends will expect you to use their first names, but if in other situations you have any doubts as to whether a first name is appropriate, start with the more formal address (i.e., Mr. Smith) and wait for the other party to insist that you call him Fred.

If somebody calls you by your first name, then you are free to use his or hers (unless you are very young or talking to a doctor who is nearly always called "Dr."). Even children regularly call adults by first name, to the dismay of many foreigners. Teachers, however, should be addressed formally, unless they insist on being called by another name.

Very few people are called by title. The exceptions are doctors and people in the military, whose rank confers a title, as in "General Powell." Police are addressed as "Officer." One might address a college professor as "Professor Harries" but a teacher is just Mr., Mrs., Miss or Ms., like nearly everybody else.

In offices nearly everybody is now on a first-name basis, including the Chief Executive Officer. But if instant familiarity makes you uncomfortable, stick to your own way. I am charmed to be called Miss Wanning.

Nicknames

Some people are universally known by their nicknames, which may or may not relate to their actual first names. Many are hold-overs from childhood. Such names as Tinky, Buzz, Butch, and Muffie are rarely on a birth certificate. A Robert is often called Bob, a William called Bill, and a Richard called Dick. A John is called Jack, a James, Jim. Other names are simple diminutives – Mike from Michael; Dan from

Daniel; Liz from Elizabeth; Art from Arthur. Then there's Hal from Harold; Steve from Stephen; Sally from Sarah.

However, many Roberts are just called Robert. You may need to ask, "Do you go by Robert, Rob or Bob?"

The latest crop of children seem to be known by nicknames much less than former generations. Presumably this is because there are fewer of them and so each one has assumed an importance too great to be reduced to a nickname. An Alexander in his crib is called Alexander; a little Benjamin is no longer known as Benny; Katherines aren't Kathy. This may also be because people are more inclined now to choose a favourite name, rather than name the child after a revered relative. So little Benjamin is not going to be confused with Uncle Benjamin, nor does he need to fill his shoes.

Conversation

It is hard to generalise about conversation in America. We have the full range of talkers – chatty, taciturn, forthcoming, secretive. Conversation is generally less lively than in the Latin countries, where everyone talks at once. When someone talks here, everyone is expected to listen, no matter how dull the talker may be. But there are countries where the conversation is far more careful and deliberate than ours.

In the search for conversational material, work is a good bet. In many countries, it is not seemly to ask, "What do you do?" Not so here. We are so often defined by our work that we are happy to talk about it. But if work proves unproductive, you might try, "What do you do in your spare time?"

We are not on the whole a reticent people. Some observers have noted that we are freer than Asians in discussing emotions and feelings, but more secretive about factual matters. Still, you can safely inquire about wives or husbands, children, geographical background, hobbies, and habits. Ethnicity is a subject of some interest, and Americans will inquire about the ancestry of others.

A highly personal conversation can take place on the basis of short acquaintance, but it will not indicate that a lasting friendship has been established. Americans can form relationships very quickly, but they don't often go deep. We constantly encounter new people we will never see again. Therefore we don't need to worry that our familiarity will entice them to become burdens to us. Airplanes are famous for inducing intimate conversations, doubtless because no follow-up is expected.

While few Americans will mind any questions you may ask – particularly if they are in the spirit of intercultural research – you may find they are delicate about asking you questions. One Chinese friend of mine says, "Americans aren't interested in other people. They don't ask questions."

My other Chinese friend says, "Ah, that's not true. They just find things out in a more roundabout manner."

We worry about invading people's privacy, and we also have the idea that foreigners aren't used to personal inquiries. So some Americans may chatter on about trivialities because they don't dare to plunge into deeper territory, but given an opening will happily take your lead. Others will resolutely talk about safe and superficial subjects until the cows come home. And still others have much to say on important but impersonal subjects, which interest them more than personal ones. (This distribution is probably not unlike the differences anywhere.)

What we have very little of are pre-cut conversational rites. Even when engaging in small talk, you have to make up your own lines.

Safe and Unsafe Subjects

You won't find Americans quick to take up the subject of religion, which is considered a personal matter. As a newcomer to the country, you could certainly ask about religious habits, but Americans who meet at parties do not inquire about each other's faiths.

Politics are discussed among people who are in relative agreement, but when a group is far apart, politics becomes a subject to be avoided. On the whole, we dislike argument. Unlike the French, who consider a verbal battle refreshing, we become personally insulted by disagreement. If an argument breaks out, we try to smooth it over or break it up.

A German who has many friends here says he is amazed how rarely the conversation turns to subjects of national or world interest. Part of the reason is that Americans are not on the whole intellectuals and are not well-informed on world matters. While it is not impolite to broach large subjects and hope for a response, you may find that conversation soon returns to harmless and painless topics. Many of these are questions of taste. Did you like such-and-such a movie? What do you think of the food at that new restaurant? Do you like Mexico? How do you like the weather? Through discussing mutual likes and dislikes, we find out whether this is our kind of person. American society is classed by tastes as much as by anything else.

Compliments are always in order. "What a pretty dress ... I love your earrings ... What a nice tie." (But not, "How much did you pay?") We keep the compliments flowing even with close friends and family. The recipient should accept the compliment graciously by looking very pleased and saying. "Oh, thank you." The tale of the item in question often provides further talk.

Most of the people you meet will be glad to hear about your country and about your impressions of America. You can be frank. We've become accustomed to criticism in recent years, although of course it's always tactful to mix a few positive comments in with the negative. ("The bus stations are awful, and I hate the food, but the people are friendly.")

There are two subjects that may rapidly bring conversation to a halt: age and money. Only as a newcomer might you plead innocent of these sanctions. If you insist on asking someone's age, it's best to lower your voice, inquire "Do you mind if I ask your age," then immediately respond with "Heavens! You look much younger!" All adult Americans are mad to look young. Actually, many of them do.

Income is a very hush-hush subject, and while we may spend a great deal of time wondering how much other people make, we don't say so. This may be because, all evidence to the contrary, we hold to the idea that people are actually paid according to their worth, and we don't care to have that figure as public knowledge.

We do not inquire about how much people paid for things either, unless we have a good reason to do so. ("I'm shopping for a new car myself. Could you tell me what that one cost you?") People who have got a great bargain are glad to volunteer the cost, but they hate to be caught overpaying.

You also should not poke too obviously into someone's class background. You do not ask, "What did your father do for a living?" To ask where someone went to college, you need a cue. ("Ah, you rowed on the Charles River; did you go to Harvard?")

Sex is, as in many cultures, best approached with discretion. Most direct questions are taboo, and probably people will grow uncomfortable if you are overly frank in presenting your own history. All appearances to the contrary, we don't take sexual matters for granted, and men who talk of their conquests are not thought very honourable. Women usually discuss methods of birth control only with close friends.

You do not inquire into someone's sexual orientation. "Are you gay?" is a forbidden question.

When all other conversation fails, there are always sports and the children to fall back on. If you are male, an interest in the fortunes of the local football and baseball teams may serve you well at parties.

Bluntness and Tact

Americans can be very direct, which may be discomfiting to people from more circuitous cultures. Here, if your neighbour thinks your apple tree is encroaching on his garden, he will tell you, rather than hint at the subject. If you claim New York is the capital of the United States, you will quickly learn you're wrong (it's Washington, D.C.).

A supervisor who thinks you're making too many mistakes will let you know.

The bluntness is somewhat tempered by language. Besides a profusion of please's and thank you's, a well-spoken person will make his points politely. "Would you mind if I borrowed your atlas?" not "Lend me your atlas." "Perhaps you could be more careful," says the supervisor to the blunderer. "I think you're a bit off there," to the person who added two and two and got five. The meaning is still clear, but a little delicacy of language leaves some respect for the other person's feelings. "I don't think you're quite right about that," goes down better than "No, you're wrong."

Criticism

Friends do not often directly criticize each other, and people who do not "mind their own business" are disdained. Even parents aghast at their grown children's behavior may choose to say nothing rather than alienate their offspring. "They have to live their own lives and make their own mistakes," say the parents with a sigh. Popular psychology insists that people's behavior comes from deep, unconscious motivations, and people can't change until they understand why they act the way they do. So, according to this theory, only a professional therapist can help them. You, their friend, would only make them angry and unhappy by offering unwanted advice.

Style of Talk

Americans admire someone who thinks fast and always has something to say. Among friends, there's apt to be a lot of cheerful banter going on. This very volubility makes some cultures distrust Americans and consider them insincere. If someone has something to say about everything, how much could she really know?

On the other hand, there are those – the French, for instance – who find Americans ponderous talkers. Ask a question, and you'll get a long-winded answer. Talk isn't lighthearted exchange for us; it's informational exchange, and we assume you want all the data you can get. In some cultures, people will take the opinion of a trusted friend. Not us. We want the facts so that we can make up our own minds. As nearly every cultural observer has noted, Americans love statistics.

What we do not like is silence. Should everyone in a group run out of things to say, an anxious pall descends until somebody saves the day by producing a subject. For the party teetering on the brink of silence (which quite a few are), almost any subject will do. By no means are all Americans slick talkers. There are those, often young males, who do not seem to have developed much verbal ability at all. Yet if you can find the right subject, they suddenly come to life. Other non-talkers may be depressed or lacking in confidence. These people often respond well to kindness and your interest in them.

Talking About Me

Compared to some peoples, we can be very boastful, and we see nothing wrong with stating our credentials frankly. However, smart conversationalists keep an edge of self-deprecation in their comments: "The company chose me to go to China so they'd have some peace in the office for a while." Or: "That was a lucky shot. I'm really a terrible golfer." You are, incidentally, not supposed to agree.

Gestures

Many Americans, eager to be understood, will use all possible means of communication, including lively gesturing with the hands and arms. The hands are intended to add emphasis and conviction, but only rarely are they lifted higher than the shoulders. Other Americans, often of Anglo-Saxon origin, do not consider gesticulation dignified and can be even somewhat wooden in their movements.

Gestures are anything but universal, sometimes bearing opposite meanings in different cultures, so the language of gestures is an important one to learn. Several of our most well-meaning signals are obscene in other countries.

157

Headshaking. Up and down is yes, and from left to right is no.

Waving. The arm is held upward, palm outward, fingers stretched out. The hand moves from side to side in a V pattern. Can mean hello or goodbye.

Snapping fingers. An attention-getting motion, not gracious, but not vulgar. May also mean, "I just remembered something." Don't snap fingers to call a waiter.

Arms folded across chest. Not rude or arrogant but could mean, "I'm waiting."

Bowing. We don't do it.

Striking forehead. Somebody who strikes his or her own forehead with an open palm is saying, "How stupid I am."

Pointing to own chest. "Do you mean me?"

Hitchhiking. Hold arm away from body, make a fist, then extend thumb. Not a vulgar gesture, as in some parts of the world.

Come here. Hold arm forward, make a fist, palm up. Extend thumb and forefinger and wiggle forefinger.

Hand wag. Fingers out and palm down. "It was so-so." Indicates lukewarm response to something.

Finger Signs
Thumb to nose. Very rude. Shows defiance.

Crossed fingers. "Good luck" or "Hope for the best." Among children, there is a code that a lie is not a lie if the fingers are crossed.

Pointing with forefinger. "Look that way."

V-sign. Either "We have won," or "We will win." Also, "Peace." Palm can face forwards or backwards.

Thumb pointed up. Success.

Thumb pointed down. Failure.

159

One or both index fingers pointed upwards from fist. "We're number one." Used mainly at sporting events.

Middle finger stuck up from fist. An obscene gesture of contempt.

Circle made with thumb and forefinger, other fingers sticking up. "Okay." "It's a go."

Telephoning

The telephone call has replaced the social call in this country. While dropping in on people uninvited is often a bad bet, you can drop in on them nearly any time via telephone. You do not, however, wish to wake up the person you're calling. If you have no idea what sort of hours somebody keeps, you should probably try not to call after 9 p.m. in the evening or before 8 a.m. in the mornings (later on weekends).

It's nice to inquire "Are you busy?" when you call. Even if you don't, callees are expected to decline to chat if the phone has rung at an inconvenient moment. They need only offer to call back. Most people have answering machines or voicemail services, and you should not hesitate to leave a message, being sure to leave your own number spoken clearly and slowly. If you receive a phone call while you have company, you should offer to call back at a mutually convenient time, even if the call is long distance.

Many foreigners could afford to work on the way they say "hello" when they answer the phone. You will notice that Americans often have a pleasant, anticipatory note (the last syllable drawn out and rising in tone) in their voices, as if they're already implying "How nice to hear from you." A dead, flat tone as in "What bill collector is bothering me now?" does not endear the caller.

Most telephone calls have some purpose. Only with very close friends do I feel free to call merely because I'm lonely or want to talk. However, I can often think of some reason ("I wondered if you knew of a good sushi restaurant?") to lift up the phone if I'm in the mood.

Now that nearly half the population has cell phones, new questions of etiquette have arisen. It is polite to turn off your cell phone when you are socialising with friends, or at least to apologize if you answer and then make the conversation very brief. Cell phone use has added an annoying new element to public life – the sound of ringing phones and people having personal conversations. Some restaurants are considering creating cell-phone-free sections, museums and libraries discourage cell-phone use, and many concerts and plays begin with reminders to turn off cell phones.

Chapter Ten

SOCIAL LIFE

ENTERTAINING

Some Americans carry on immensely busy social lives, and others live in virtual isolation. Some spend most of their time with their families, and others see almost everybody except their families. Some people love parties, and some hate them.

Social class is a determinant here. The upper classes, having more time and money at their disposal than most, entertain and visit a great deal. The lower classes, less mobile and lacking space for large parties, are more apt to limit their social lives to church suppers and their families.

It's the middle classes that get headaches over entertaining. It's for them that magazines run endless articles about party food, serving, decorating, and manners. The articles serve only to fuel middle class American anxiety over being hosts and hostesses.

We have the impression that the good life involves lots of gay parties, but entertaining doesn't come naturally to many of us. It's not only a lot of work, it's stressful.

The magazines and TV cooking shows have convinced us that "an informal dinner" requires very out-of-the-ordinary preparations – elegant foods, special wines, flower arrangements, a clean house. This is a lot of work (if you have no servants) just in order to sit around and talk.

Some people love to cook, but many are acutely aware that they have nothing in their repertoires that will do for parties. We are at a disadvantage because the dishes we were brought up on (roast beef, fried chicken) are neither healthy nor gourmet. So we must pore over cookbooks making up the menu, shop at specialty markets, and arduously follow the small print of the recipes. Lining up the guests can be a challenge too as many people have their Saturday evenings, the most usual night for a dinner party, scheduled weeks in advance.

The truth is many Americans really don't enjoy this form of socialising. It's set, strained, difficult, and most of our friends are not such brilliant conversationalists that it seems worth the bother.

Why a Party?

Nonetheless, entertain we must. It's a requirement of middle-class life, and people who don't fulfil it feel guilty and are constantly muttering, "We must have the so-and-so's over." A party may be given in celebration of an occasion (birthday, wedding, graduation) or to honour a visitor, but more commonly takes place for no other reason than "the fun of it."

A generation or two ago, company wives were expected to entertain in order to boost their husbands' careers; now that many wives are more interested in their own careers, the business dinner is likely to take place in a restaurant. Business gatherings have an advantage in that people are doing what they really like best: working. But aside from business, there are still any number of reasons for throwing a party.

If nothing else, one wants to show off the house. The average American is obsessed with home decorating and after having spent a large amount of time and money in fixing up the place, it's nice to have people come and admire the results (do try to say nice things about people's homes when you visit). After all, we discourage people from dropping in (partly because we don't like to be caught with a messy house) so what is the large living room for?

Another motivation for having parties is that our families are often either physically far apart or spiritually distant. A gathering of friends is an attempt to fill the empty place left by the dispersal of the clan. No one wants to feel alone in the universe. We may not want friends to take up too much of our time, but we do want to have them. A big party is an efficient way to keep in touch with scattered acquaintances. And of course, party obligations and social debts must be returned if one wishes to continue to have a social life.

The Guests

Visitors from afar may be surprised at how homogeneous the guests are at even a large gathering – no old mothers or dotty uncles or children. People tend to socialise with their own age groups. Children have children's parties; old people have old people's parties. If you find otherwise, you have probably happened in on a family party, or have arrived in rural circles.

This homogeneity of age, however, does not necessarily assist the conversational flow. Because Americans move around and change jobs so much, many of them do not belong to any particular social circle, and their various friends often do not know each other. In fact, the hosts themselves sometimes barely know their guests. They round up their disparate acquaintances in the optimistic hope that some party magic will take over and make the fun.

Too often, conversation falls flat or becomes hard work. We have all at one time or another found ourselves in a room full of strangers looking desperately for a friendly face to talk to. Few hosts find time to do a proper job of introducing people to each other. Under such circumstances, don't hesitate to bluntly introduce yourself. "Hello, I'm Lakshmi Karna," followed by "How do you know the hosts?" are acceptable opening lines from which further conversation can usually be developed.

Other parties consist entirely of the troops from the office. On these occasions an air of discomfort can also fall, resulting from the general sense that it's inappropriate to discuss business at a party, but unnatural to discuss the weather and such with people one sees every day. In the end, business usually wins out, and then everybody relaxes.

Although such office parties take place, it is not considered necessary to entertain work colleagues. People who are inseparable in the office may have never been to each other's homes. An Indian confided, "When I first came here, I was terribly offended that the people I met at work didn't invite me home. Later, I was glad because I wanted to have time to myself too." For better or worse, our busy lives tend to be compartmentalized.

Once you've accepted an invitation to a party, you must attend. If something happens to prevent you, telephone with your excuses as soon as possible. People work hard to give a party; you must remember that it's nearly always your hosts, not the servants, who have spent the day cooking and cleaning, and they could be very upset if you don't show up. Furthermore, other guests may have been invited specifically to meet you.

Having Fun ?

A Chinese man says that what strikes him about American parties is that people rarely seem to be having an awfully good time. I think this is a fair observation. There's a lot of onus involved in being an American – that is, in being individually responsible for one's fate and it doesn't fly away at a party. We don't arrive surrounded by a family or a culture that makes us feel secure, and the party itself may seem like another test – new people to meet and impress. Some people use alcohol to remove their inhibitions, but many prefer to cope without both the high spirits and the hangover. My Irish friend thinks that American parties are simply too civilised. This is not to say that all American parties are grim. Most are quite pleasant, and some are positively jubilant.

Actually, despite any generalisations I may make, there's a large element of surprise in an American party. The old rules for entertaining have been thrown out, and new ones haven't replaced them. Americans may be as bemused as you are at the form the evening takes. Will the hosts be wearing dress suits or ragged jeans? Will the meal be served as soon as one walks in the door or hours later? Will loud music substitute for conversation? Will the other guests be fascinating and friendly or otherwise? Who knows? Perhaps the hosts will arrive home with the bags of groceries while you're standing on the doorstep. Visitors from abroad, at least, can chalk it all up to cultural experience.

More and more people have just given up on the whole effort and meet friends at restaurants. This is an acceptable option.

The Dinner Party

The invitation will probably come by telephone. You needn't say yes or no on the spot ("I'll have to check with my husband and make sure we're free" is standard), but you should provide an answer as soon as possible. If you are married, you can assume that your spouse is invited; unless specified, your children are not. If you are living with a "significant other," that person is usually invited, but it's up to you to make sure that your host knows that the person exists. What you should not do is show up with an unexpected guest – no matter how informal the occasion.

The dress code for a dinner party can be unpredictable, and it's not only foreigners who are puzzled by it. The problem is that there are very few conventions remaining.

People who wear a white shirt and tie to work every day may greet you at the door in jeans. But if they're older, formal, or coming from work, they could be wearing suits. Among very good friends there's little dressing up, and at a middle class get-together, you are likely to find gentlemen without ties but wearing good-looking sweaters and slacks. Party wear often consists of looking as if you made an effort for your hosts' sake without forsaking the casual look altogether. A jacket with a turtleneck is generally a safe bet for most occasions.

Women often dress up much more than men – perhaps because there are few opportunities left to wear a pretty dress. At any rate, a woman can always wear dressy pants with a blouse and fit in anywhere. In America, a skirt is more elegant, and more formal, than pants. If you are suffering any doubts as to what to wear, simply ask your hosts, "Is it dressy?"

Protocol

You don't need to walk in the door on the dot of the time you were invited for, but you should arrive within 10 to 20 minutes afterwards. If you're much later, your hosts may grow anxious. American dinner food is usually ready at a particular time and gets overcooked or cold with waiting. At some houses, though, it doesn't matter when you arrive because a long cocktail hour will precede dinner. However, as one rarely knows which houses these are, if you are going to be more than half an hour late you should telephone and say so. Whatever you do, don't arrive early.

The old etiquette was to serve dinner 45 minutes after the time of the invitation, and this is still a good rule of thumb. It is customary to offer people a drink as soon as they arrive. "What'll you have to drink?" says the host. "What have you got?" is the usual answer.

There is no need for the hosts to provide everything anyone might want. They may reasonably offer only wine, beer, and soft drinks. Some people put out elaborate hors d'oeuvres (appetizers), while others prefer that their guests save their appetites for dinner.

At Table

If the dinner is the least bit formal, guests will be ushered to a dining table to eat. They should hesitate before grabbing seats and ask the hostess where she would like them to sit. If she is a very vigilant hostess she will have calculated places in advance, probably putting men between women. There is also a fading custom that the place of honour for a man is on the hostess's right and that of a woman on the host's right. Your hosts may say, "Oh, sit anywhere," in which case you may be able to manipulate yourself into a seat next to someone you think you would like to talk to. At any rate, men should not all huddle at one end of the table, leaving the women at the other end.

Don't start eating until everyone has been served. A few families say grace before meals, which is a thank you to God for the food (such as: "Lord, we ask you to bless this food to our use and ourselves to thy service. Amen.") It is embarrassing to be caught with your spoon in your mouth when grace is being said and your head should be bowed. It is nice to repeat "Amen" at the end of the grace.

You may or may not have soup to start, followed by a main course (fish, meat, or perhaps pasta or a casserole) with vegetables. Salad may come before, with, or after the main course. A fattening dessert and coffee generally ends the meal. (*See* "Table Manners" *in Chapter Six for details on using the silverware*).

Asians and Middle Easterners sometimes go away hungry from American tables because they consider it polite to refuse food when it is first offered. Here, if you say you do not want more, your hosts will believe you and probably will not urge you further. When hosts offer more food, they like their guests to immediately say, "Yes, please. It's delicious." They also like guests who eat everything on

169

their plates. If you fail to, you should explain that good as the food is, you are too full to finish.

Dinner party conversation is often punctuated with exclamations about how delicious the food is. We do not take for granted that someone can cook and tend to rhapsodise whether they do it very well or not. The rest of the conversation may be wide-ranging. It's important to keep it going, and your efforts will be appreciated. Nothing is worse than a dinner at which the party eats in silence. Be sure to address your remarks equally to the men and women at the table. Women are as educated and well-read as men and resent not being considered equal conversationalists.

Departing

You should not leave immediately after dinner; doing so would suggest that you could hardly wait to leave. You must let a certain conversational period elapse, and then you should make excuses for going at all. You may, for instance, suddenly look at your watch and say, "Good heavens, look at the time. We really must leave." Or, "Whew, past my bedtime. Early game of golf tomorrow." You should do this before your hosts begin to yawn visibly and look threateningly at you. Staying too late is almost as bad as leaving too early. Your hosts still have the dishes to do. If you are not out by 11 p.m., they probably have cause for complaint, and many parties break up earlier. Should your hosts object vigorously when you start to leave and beg you to stay longer, do – but only if you want to. Before departing, say good night to the other guests, expressing your pleasure at having seen or met them.

It is excellent manners to telephone the next day and offer further thanks for the fine time you had, but not everybody does. If you prefer, a note of thanks (even a postcard) is just as good as a phone call – or even better as it takes very little of your time and none of the host's.

Some people may enjoy your company enough to ask you repeatedly to dinner without a return move on your part, but usually you are

Three generations of a family gather for cocktails at their summer home.

expected to return the hospitality before being invited back again. This is a convenient custom because if you are not anxious to continue the relationship, you can simply fail to reciprocate. However, if you want to pay them back in some other way, you can send flowers, or invite your friends to a restaurant or to the theatre.

Cocktail Parties

This drinking institution was lagging in popularity a short time ago but is now making a comeback. The cocktail party does have a solid contribution to make to social life as it allows the hosts to entertain a large number of people in a small amount of time. It's largely a stand-up institution so you can invite as many people as you can pack vertically into your house. Very often an invitation will give both start and finish times, for instance 5–7 p.m. In reality, unless the hosts are rushing off to the theatre, a 5–7 party would probably go on until at least 8, but guests should arrive by 6:30 p.m. anyhow. Cocktail parties are apt to be a bit dressier than other kinds of parties, perhaps because they've survived mainly in old-fashioned circles.

171

Some cocktail parties will offer only a few potato chips and olives to eat. Others have lavish, delectable displays that substitute nicely for dinner. At a buffet table, you help yourself without waiting for an invitation from your hosts.

Americans are demonstrably drinking less than formerly, and most of your guests will probably drink wine, beer, or soft drinks. A hot, non-alcoholic punch I once made was surprisingly popular. But you should still have hard liquor on hand at a cocktail party (unless you have religious or moral objections to alcohol in which case you might better give a tea party) – gin, bourbon, scotch, and vodka along with the so-called set-ups (tonic, soda, lime, and plenty of ice). Some people add pizazz to their parties by mixing martinis or some other fancy cocktail they favor.

You should know that if someone drinks too much at your house and has a car accident on the way home, you could be held responsible. If any of your guests do get drunk (and it should certainly not be because you forced drinks upon them), do not allow them to drive. Either keep them with you, drive them home yourself, get someone else to drive them home, or send for a taxi.

The Potluck

This bring-your-own-dish party is an old American custom. Its origins lie in the church social, when a large group would gather for an informal supper, each family bringing a dish. Organizations often have potlucks, and some individuals do too; you may be invited to bring your share of the food to anything from a brunch to a wedding. Such a gathering is usually extremely informal, and you needn't be as precise about whether or not you're attending as for a dinner party (unless it is a wedding).

Some potlucks are so casual that the invitation – often a photocopied sheet sent to practically everyone the party-giver knows – does not even require a reply. But usually there's an RSVP (which is French for "answer please"), and whenever you see RSVP you should reply as soon as possible. You may be instructed in the kind of dish to bring, but if not it is polite, though not obligatory, to ask. It is also helpful if you announce beforehand what you plan to bring. Some people arrive with just a bottle or two of wine, but obviously it would not be a good thing if everybody did that.

The drawback of potlucks, besides having to bring a dish that nobody may eat, is their unpredictability. Most have far too much food (your dish need only be large enough for one course for four people – or the equivalent of one person eating four courses), but I've been to a few where the table was practically bare or the choice was limited to varieties of pasta salad. Some potlucks, however, garner a wonderful array of delectable dishes.

A potluck is much looser in terms of arrival and departure time than the dinner party. Usually eating goes on throughout the party so your dish may be consumed even if you arrive late. It's good to bring something relatively simple from the eating point of view. You can count on plates and forks being available, but if you're bringing soup you'd better bring the bowls too. The casualness of potlucks extends also to dress. It's a rare potluck that requires a suit.

Some foreigners are appalled by the very idea of potlucks. "What's the point," asks a Chinese man, "to invite people to dinner and to tell them to bring the food?" Potlucks are more often than not thrown by people who are genuinely sociable, but who don't want to spend days cooking for a large crowd. They would say that eating isn't the point of a party anyhow, it's the company.

The Barbecue

A barbecue is where American hosts come into their own. All you need is a back yard and a grill; the informality suits us well. There's nothing President Bush likes better than to have his guests down to a real Texas barbecue at his ranch. Barbecue meats vary greatly by region, and in the South the barbecue sauce makes or breaks the cook's reputation. However, at the standard suburban barbecue, any kind of meat that can be cooked on a grill will do.

Barbecuing is a manly art, and it's your host who you will find behind the grill. Your hostess will bring out the side dishes – salads and bread. Dessert may be pie, cake or ice cream.

The Brunch

Brunch is a Sunday morning affair that combines breakfast and lunch, held anywhere between 10 a.m. and 2 p.m. The meal imitates breakfast, usually featuring juice, fruit salad, pastries, and eggs, but anything is possible. Champagne or Bloody Marys (tomato juice and vodka) are often on the menu.

Dress is usually casual/pretty. It is Sunday morning (churchgoing time) so you want to look nice. But degree of dressiness depends on the place and the hosts. An attractive jogging suit could be the thing.

The After-Dinner Party

This is apt to be an anything-goes party. Dress up or dress down, come early or late. The party probably won't be in full swing until quite late in the evening. Loud music may inspire dancing. There will certainly be drinks; food may be scarce or it may be abundant. Try to find your hosts to thank before going home.

Birthday Parties

An adult birthday, unless it's one of some significance, such as 21, 40, 50, 60 or 75, is usually just an excuse for having a party and doesn't need special recognition. You could bring a little present, but there's no need to.

For a children's birthday, however, you must come with a present. The price category is tricky. A bag of balloons would look cheap next to other presents, but a remote control car would be far too extravagant. Parents have an unspoken agreement not to go broke on kids' birthday presents and look with disfavour at those parents who overspend. Fortunately, children don't love presents according to their price tags.

Where parents often try to outdo each other is in laying on the entertainment for Junior's party. There are those who hire clowns and ponies and caterers and magicians or else sweep the children away to fancy clubs, theatre matinees, etc. While this is all very nice (if ostentatious), children remain extremely happy playing the traditional party games – pin-the-tail-on-the-donkey, spider's web, blind man's bluff, musical chairs, etc. – followed by ice cream and cake. The Latin influence from south of the border has brought the piñata to North America; any games you can introduce from your culture will add a memorable note. In fact, if you give your child a birthday party just like the one you would give back home, it will doubtless be a hit. If you're intent on the American kind, greeting card shops or big drugstores often sell booklets that tell how to run a traditional children's birthday party.

RECREATION

Going out to movies and restaurants are central pastimes for many. There are people who rent a movie nearly every night to watch on their VCRs or DVD players. But probably nobody's time is as fully occupied as that of the true sports fan.

Spectator Sports

Many American men are deeply involved with sports. This does not necessarily mean that they play any of them. What they do is watch national teams on television. There are men who follow baseball, football, basketball, hockey, golf, and tennis – which requires them to be in front of the television set for the better part of any weekend. If they are sociable, their buddies may be watching with them. There are plenty of female sports fans too, but not many women feel as free as men to give up their weekends to watching sports.

Photo: Esther Wanning

Baseball is the great American unifier and has followers in all income and ethnic groups. Nearly every major city has a team, and as each team plays 162 games a year, following baseball can be time-consuming. The season occupies spring and summer and culminates in the fall World Series, during which the two leading teams play each other. The first to win four games wins the Series. Although called the "World" Series, Canada is the only other country to participate.

Football, played in fall and winter, also has a powerful hold on the country. It should not be confused with the game called "football" elsewhere, which we call "soccer." There is very little kicking in our football, which has more to do with running with the ball and knocking people down. Serious injuries are common in football. Each team only plays 16 games during the regular season, and these take place on Sundays and Monday evenings.

Super-Bowl Sunday, the final football playoff in January, finds half the country glued to the television set, although if the local team is not in the finals, the passion is muted. Friends gather together in front of the largest television in the crowd. Quantities of beer are swilled, and platefuls of food passed around. The food is of the easily eaten variety – hot dogs, potato chips, cold cuts, bread, salads – so that people can fix, eat, and watch all at once.

Professional teams, which include basketball and ice hockey teams, are expected to be profitable for their owners, and they certainly are for the television networks. The games allow plenty of time for commercials.

Soccer is of growing importance among schoolchildren in America, and is also now played on the national level. A professional league is well-established, and although game attendance remains comparatively low, cable channels (particularly Spanish stations) find it worthwhile to provide coverage. Still, people who follow world soccer are good candidates to buy satellite dishes.

College sports occupy the television screens when nothing else does. Christmas and New Year's Day are devoted to college football. The big universities, which avidly recruit promising players from high schools, are invariably the winners. Whether college players should be intellectually capable is an ongoing debate in the sports world. Many colleges feel that if they want their alumni to donate generously to their old school, they need a winning football team. Curiously enough, this seems to be true.

Some adults continue to play baseball after high school and college on amateur teams sponsored by cities, towns, and companies. Although these games are supposed to be purely for fun, foreigners may be surprised at how seriously they are taken. Americans care a great deal about winning.

Active Sports

Not every American man hunts and fishes, but many more do than in the world at large. We have some wild country and fairly clear streams left, and our frontier days, when hunting and eating were intimately entwined, were not so long ago. There are still rural families who count on bagging their annual deer to get through the winter. Most current hunting, however, is for the sport – the opportunity to be outdoors stalking living things through swamp, bush, stream, or woods.

177

Going fishing with the fellows represents heaven to many American males.

Fishing is popular with a large cross-section of the population, and unlike in England, "shooting" is not a particularly upper class pursuit. The elite may ride to the hounds, but families with racks of rifles over the fireplace are not usually the heirs to old money.

The rich have often rechanneled their killing instincts and are satisfied to go out with their tennis rackets and golf clubs to expensive country clubs. Tennis and golf, however, are by no means restricted to the monied classes. Public golf courses can be inexpensive and public tennis courts are usually free.

Sailing, motor-boating, windsurfing, hang-gliding, skiing, kayaking, snow-mobiling, mountain-climbing, water-skiing, and hiking are a few other avocations that allow Americans to exert themselves outdoors. Many people feel the need to have the best and newest equipment for each sport.

Formal Dancing

Just when it seemed that the only waltz any of us would ever see would be in reruns of *War and Peace,* old-fashioned dancing is back with a vengeance. Check listings in your local paper, and you're apt to find classes and evenings of salsa, tango, rumba, swing, waltz, fox trot, folk dances of many kinds and more. All ages are enthusiasts, and partners often aren't required.

High Culture

"What struck me most about the United States when I first came was sex and money," said a Japanese man. He meant by that the importance assigned to both – the bombardment of sexual imagery in advertising and the lust for money.

In the midst of this unrefined landscape, you would not expect much high culture, but in fact the USA shines in many of the arts. There is, however, a great gulf between high culture (classical music, ballet, opera, museum art) and mass culture (movies, television, popular music, hotel art). A small proportion of the public support the museums, opera houses, symphonies, chamber groups, and dance companies.

Nonetheless, the arts are thriving and the calibre of performances high. Most of the financial backing comes from private individuals and foundations, rather than from the government. In the past decade, many of the Western and Southern cities, which were long considered cultural wastelands, have developed top-flight artistic programs. Recent immigrants contribute greatly to the pool of talent.

HOLIDAYS

Each holiday has its own particular flavour, but most of them only arouse excitement in so far as they provide an excuse for a holiday from work or school. Only Christmas and Thanksgiving inspire great expectations. Whether you think the USA has a lot of holidays or very few depends on where you come from.

179

The Major Holidays

CHRISTMAS: "Tis the season to be jolly," says the Christmas song. December 25 remembers the birth of Christ and is the biggest holiday of the year. Its celebration goes far beyond its religious origins, and most of the festivities have little to do with religion. In fact, the holiday may originally have been a pagan celebration of the winter solstice (December 21), when the days start to get longer again.

Christmas calls people home from far away to be with their families, and each family has its own Christmas rituals. Although Jews and members of some other religions may prefer not to, most houses have a decorated Christmas tree, and people cook (or buy) special foods for the season – Christmas cookies, plum puddings, fruitcakes. Everybody is expected to have a family or family substitute at Christmas time; it is the only time of year that some families see each other. It is also a particularly depressing time of year for those who are alone.

The central ritual of Christmas is the exchanging of gifts which are intended to represent the "goodwill towards men" that Christ preached. Every year, voices rise to protest the insane commercialism of Christmas, but nothing has dimmed the enthusiasm for gift-giving. As a nation of shameless consumers a holiday centred around shopping suits us very well.

Charitable giving is at a peak at Christmas as well. "Blessed are the poor," said Christ, and so it's a time of year when many people feel inclined to brighten the lives of the less fortunate. An abundance of fine dinners are offered to the poor and homeless on Christmas; the charitable institutions try to emphasise that the need goes on all year.

CHRISTMAS MERRYMAKING: A fair proportion of the year's parties are given at Christmas time. As Christmas takes place the week before the new year begins, the holiday spirit does not diminish even after Christmas. Christmas parties can be given any time between December

Santa Claus is seen everywhere at Chnstmastime. Little children are told that on the night before Chnstmas while they are asleep, he comes down the chimney with presents for good children.

6 and December 29. "Open Houses" are popular, some given on Christmas Eve or Christmas Day.

Family traditions vary. Some people open their presents on Christmas Eve, and some wait until Christmas Day. There are many church services on Christmas Eve; Midnight Mass is popular (usually held at 11 p.m.). Throughout the Christmas season there is much singing of Christmas carols, lovely songs well known to most Americans. Special concerts play Christmas music, and Handel's *Messiah* can be heard everywhere.

Usually a big dinner makes its way to the family table sometime between 1 p.m. and 7 p.m. on Christmas Day. You, as a foreigner, for whom everyone will feel sorry if you are far from family, may well be invited to one of these. You may wish to bring a bottle of wine or

Photo: The Weekly Packet

champagne or flowers or a potted plant – the poinsettia is the Christmas flower.

NEW YEAR'S EVE: Our calendar elects January 1 as the first day of the new year. The big celebrations are held the evening of December 31. Parties should be gala, and you are supposed to drink champagne and kiss everybody at midnight. Some of us prefer to go to bed at 11 p.m. and start the new year well rested, but the young and romantic feel that on this night of nights they must have a date and preferably be in love. New Year's Day, January 1, is subject to a round of Open Houses but can properly be celebrated very quietly – nursing a hangover or in making grandiose New Year resolutions (such as giving up smoking or losing weight).

While most companies only give workers a day or two off at Christmas, it's a time when many people take personal vacation days.

The week before Christmas and New Year's Day is not a time any one should seriously expect to get much business done. Those of your business partners who haven't flown to the homes of distant relatives may be in the mountains skiing or in the tropics swimming. Not everything grinds to a halt, but you are unlikely to find a full quorum of decision makers on the scene.

THANKSGIVING: The fourth Thursday of November, Americans celebrate Thanksgiving and remember a supposed feast between the Indians and the Pilgrims in 1621. Had the Indians not befriended the Pilgrims during that winter, the Pilgrims would have starved. In recognition of this alliance (and ignoring all the bloodshed that followed) and of the success of the Mayflower settlement, Americans have a harvest feast.

A big turkey (wild turkey was an Indian delicacy) is central to Thanksgiving. Surrounding the turkey, one expects to see stuffing,

Photo: Esther Wanning

The members of this family have flown in from all parts of the country to be together for Thanksgiving.

183

cranberry sauce, potatoes, squash, and pumpkin and mincemeat pies. Whether or not the Pilgrims enjoyed the same foods, these dishes are all New England specialties that grace nearly every table at Thanksgiving.

It is as important to have somewhere to go on Thanksgiving as it is on Christmas. Some businesses are closed both on Thanksgiving, a Thursday, and the next day, a Friday, enabling people to travel great distances to join their families. However, other than wishing others a Happy Thanksgiving, Thanksgiving is not nearly as demanding as Christmas. No gifts or celebrating other than the dinner itself are required. It is a generous holiday, and many families welcome those who haven't a family of their own nearby.

The Minor Holidays

The significance of the minor holidays is mainly the long weekend they provide – many are observed not on their actual date but on a handy federally mandated Monday. A few of them are marked with parades, but the only celebration for most people is in sleeping late. Not all of them provide even that. On many of these holidays the ordinary worker works, but banks, schools, and government offices are closed. Stores are usually open and often have big holiday sales.

New Year's Day: January 1. Businesses closed. A popular time to hold an Open House.

Martin Luther King Day: January 16, the birthday of the great civil rights' leader, celebrated on the closest Monday. The degree of observance varies from one city and state to the next. Often a school and government holiday, but most businesses are open.

Presidents' Day: The birthdays of Abraham Lincoln (February 12) and George Washington (February 20) are combined in one convenient mid-February Monday, awarding a welcome long weekend in the middle of winter. Theoretically, Franklin Roosevelt is included in the celebration, but few people realise it.

Valentine's Day: St. Valentine was the patron saint of lovers, and on

February 14, people give cards, candy, and flowers to loved ones. Children often give cards to everyone they know. Not an official holiday.

Easter: A Christian holiday celebrating the day that Jesus rose from the dead. Children color Easter eggs and have Easter egg hunts and often receive chocolate bunny rabbits or baskets of candy and toys. The date falls on a Sunday anywhere between late March and late April. Easter heralds the beginning of spring.

Mother's Day: The second Sunday of May. A day to pay tribute to Mother, with cards, flowers, and restaurant dinners.

Memorial Day: A national holiday on the last Monday of May; commemorates the Americans who have died in war and kicks off summer. A good day for a picnic.

Father's Day: The third Sunday of June. Not as important as

Photo: The Weekly Packet

A Memorial Day parade in a small town brings out anyone who has served the country in the armed forces and still has a uniform to wear. Many flags are waved.

185

Mother's Day, but still the fifth largest card-sending occasion.

Fourth of July: A national holiday. On July 4, 1776, the Declaration of Independence was signed. Also called Independence Day, it's another good picnic day. Official celebrations consist of fireworks displays; most private fireworks are now illegal, but many people set them off anyhow.

Labor Day: The first Monday in September and the occasion for the last picnic of summer; a day of honour (and rest) for the worker. The school year traditionally starts a day or two after Labor Day.

Columbus Day: October 12, the day in 1492 when Christopher Columbus landed in the New World.

Halloween: October 31, the evening that children put on costumes and go out 'Trick or Treating,' which means that if you don't provide treats when they knock on your door, they will enact a dirty trick on you (such as writing on your windows with soap). It's a good idea to stock up on some Halloween candy (wrapped) to hand out, but you probably don't really need to worry about the tricks. It's the parents who do the worrying now – that some atrocious person will give their child poisoned food. For this reason, parents usually supervise their children's rounds very closely.

Veterans' Day: November 11. Honors those who have served their country in the armed services.

SPECIAL OCCASIONS

New Babies

It is customary for a friend to give a "baby shower" for an expectant mother. Traditionally, only other women are invited, and each arrives with a present for the baby, prettily wrapped. The usual routine is for the party to begin with refreshments and chat, followed by the opening of the presents. The women sit in a circle and the mother-to-be opens the presents one by one amidst oohs and aahs. Baby books, bonnets, little stretch suits, toys, blankets, and anything else a baby might want are all appropriate. A handmade item is especially appreciated.

There is no particular custom for visiting after the baby is born. Good friends might arrange to stop in a week or more after the birth, bearing a present if they haven't already contributed one at the shower. As new parents are harried and have little time to cook, they will be grateful if you bring them something for their dinner.

CHRISTENING: A ceremony at which a baby is named and received into the Church, usually as part of Sunday morning services. If you're invited to one of these, just do what everyone else does, and don' t be insulted if you're not invited – usually only relatives are.

Birthdays

Except for children's birthday parties, most birthday celebrations are kept within the family. Usually each family member gives a present to the birthday person. Children count on birthdays and Christmas as the times to get the big things they really want, such as new bicycles.

A home celebration consists of a special dinner, ending with ice cream and cake. For children, each candle on the cake represents one year of life, and everyone sings, "Happy birthday to you," when the cake appears with candles lit. The honoree then makes a wish and tries to blow out all the candles at once.

Weddings

The traditional American wedding was rocked by the sixties and emerged in a variety of new forms. It became popular for couples to write their own vows and to add a variety of personal touches to the proceedings. Nonetheless, many of the old customs survive, even if in an updated form, and some couplings are more tradition-bound than ever before.

The most important thing to know about weddings is that you must arrive on time. This is an occasion when the guests should appear before the hosts; it is most embarrassing to arrive after the bride has already walked down the aisle. As wedding ceremonies start on time and are usually very short, you may miss the main event entirely by being late.

THE CLASSIC CHURCH WEDDING: When the American girl dreams of her wedding, she probably sees herself wafting down a church aisle on her father's arm, radiant in a long white dress.

You as a guest are occupying a pew in the church. When the processional music begins and the first members of the wedding party are visible, the congregation rises to its feet. Ushers, bridesmaids, and flower girls lead the procession, and the bride and her father bring up the rear. The groom, best man, and minister slip in quietly to their positions in front.

The minister begins, "Dearly beloved, we are gathered here together to join this man and woman in matrimony..." After his opening, the groom steps in to the father's place. (Modern variations remove the implication that the bride is a piece of livestock being given from the father to the husband.) Rings are exchanged – to be worn on the fourth finger of the left hand – and the ritual questions asked, "Do you take this man to be your husband/wife, to have and to hold, to love and to cherish, in sickness and in health, till death do you part?"

By this time many in the audience are becoming weepy and getting out their handkerchiefs. The minister concludes with, "I now pronounce you husband and wife," the organist breaks into Mendelssohn's *Wedding March* and the happy couple sweeps joyfully back down the aisle, with the wedding party trailing afterwards.

The congregation departs, falling into the arms of long-lost relatives on the way out, and all go off to the reception.

THE VARIATIONS: The above describes the standard Protestant ceremony. A Jewish service is somewhat different, and a Catholic Mass

Photo: Bambi Smith for Don Gerhardt Photography

At a formal wedding such as this, the bride and groom are "attended" by bridesmaids and ushers. It is an honor to be chosen to take part, one extended to brothers, sisters, and close friends.

a great deal longer. Similar proceedings can take place in gardens, homes, and hotels. Often a justice of the peace presides, removing the religious factor.

The simplest wedding of all is the City Hall version: the couple and a few witnesses appear before a judge and are married.

THE RECEPTION: Here's where the money goes. There are means of spending lavish sums on a wedding reception. The caterers get the largest share, followed by expenditures for reception rooms, champagne, flowers, photographers, orchestra, printed napkins, and countless other little touches. Some families go into debt for years to pay off their daughters' weddings. (Tradition has it that the bride's family pays for the wedding, although increasingly – now that people wait longer to get married – couples finance and arrange their own.)

189

There is no disgrace, however, in a party at home with food supplied by the relatives. There are those who consider the small home garden party more charming than the no-holds-barred hotel affairs usually directed by a bossy photographer.

If there is a receiving line, etiquette demands that you pass through it. You kiss the bride (if you know her) and tell her she looks beautiful, and you shake the groom's hand and tell him he's a lucky man. You tell the bride's mother how moved you were by the ceremony, and you make a little joke to the bride's father about not having to pay his daughter's bills any more.

You have now done your duty and may drink champagne and circulate and join in the festivities, which usually start with food and drink and move on to dancing. When the orchestra strikes up, protocol demands that the bride and groom dance the first dance alone and the second with their parents. After the parents have danced, the rest of the guests may join in. When the word goes around that the bride and groom are going to cut the cake, everyone pulls close for a look at their first cooperative married venture. You must eat at least a bit of the cake for good luck.

Properly speaking, you should not leave before the bridal couple does – although if it looks as if they're not going anywhere you needn't wait forever. The old standard is for the bride to disappear somewhere, then to reappear in her travelling clothes. Preferably from some balcony or staircase she throws her bouquet to a young unmarried woman – who may expect to be the next to be wed – and departs on the arm of her groom, amid showers of rice (a fertility rite). Today, however, many couples prefer to enjoy their parties to the end.

PRESENTS: An old-fashioned custom was to display wedding presents received before the wedding at the reception, but most people no longer consider showing off "the loot" tasteful. You may bring your present to the wedding (it won't be opened until later), but most couples would prefer you mailed it to their home address.

Theoretically, one is allotted a year after the wedding in which to send a present, although most people don't wait that long. Cash is not quite as frequently given here as in some countries, although it is often most welcome. If you are uncertain, you might inquire from relatives as to the couple's wishes. Should the couple already have a house groaning with toasters and china, it may be that there is nothing they would like better than money.

But cash (make it a cheque) should not be your first thought. The traditional wedding present is a handsome household item – anything from a good frying pan to a crystal punch bowl. Some brides register their desires at a prominent local store. Having found out where the bride is registered, you then need only appear there and pick out whatever is in your price range. Shopping at prominent stores in general has the advantage that the couple may easily return your present if they don't like it or if it's a duplicate.

Price should not be affected by the lavishness of the wedding reception – but often you can't help but feel that you should at least cover the cost of your dinner. The real determinants of price should be your fondness and goodwill towards the couple, their needs, and how much you have to spend. A well chosen gift of low cost will arouse delight among decent people. And if your own resources are small, the couple should feel badly should you spend more than you can afford.

If you are invited to a wedding and cannot attend, you are not obligated to send a present – although you may wish to. (You must, however, mail your regrets as soon as possible.) Likewise, if you receive an announcement after the fact of the wedding, a gift is entirely optional.

Quite promptly after sending your present, you should receive a thank-you note, giving specific and personal reasons as to why the couple was so delighted with your present. To not acknowledge a wedding present is unforgivable.

Funerals

These too come in a variety of forms. Most frequently, they are held in churches or funeral homes. You should wear sombre, proper clothes (such as a dark suit with a sober tie for men and a prim dress or suit for women) and arrive looking reasonably solemn.

An usher will guide you to a seat. The service will probably be between a half-hour and an hour long. Many funerals now include testimonials from friends, but unless you have been solicited beforehand, you will not be required to speak, although you may be given the opportunity.

American funerals sometimes display an open casket and provide an opportunity for the attendees to file by and pay their last respects to the departed. You may find your friend remarkably changed in death, probably due to the morticians, who go to such lengths to make the dead face look serene that he or she may be unrecognizable.

During the funeral, you may sob all you like but you should not lose control or cry out loud. Unless you are next of kin, you do not wish to draw attention to yourself and your grief.

You may have an opportunity to greet family members after the funeral, whereupon you convey how sorry you are and how greatly the deceased will be missed. Sometimes there has also been an opportunity to call in at the funeral home on preceding evenings to console the family. There may be a graveside ceremony after the church service, which usually includes only family and close friends. Unless you are specifically invited, you should go home.

There may instead be a reception or a wake, likewise by special invitation. This may turn into a very jolly party, but you should try to do your part in keeping the focus on the departed – with stories and reminiscences of his or her uniqueness. It is sometimes hard to remember the sadness of the occasion when a number of long-lost friends and relatives gather together, and a certain amount of mirth is excused.

Death is not an occasion for monetary contributions to the family.

Close friends and relatives may send flowers and wreaths for display at the funeral; often the family requests contributions to a certain charity instead.

If someone you know dies and you do not have an opportunity to speak to the bereaved family, you should write a note or send a sympathy card. Even if you attend the funeral, a note to family members reiterating your sorrow is thoughtful.

Dying

If you should suffer a death in your own family while in this country, be very wary of funeral homes, which are famous for charging astronomically for unnecessary services. Although it is not a time when one cares to be thinking about finances, it is unlikely that your loved one would wish you to bankrupt yourself for something he or she will not enjoy. So think twice about whether you really need a mahogany, velvet-lined coffin, etc.

BANQUETS

All kinds of clubs and civic organisations find excuses to have banquets so you may well find yourself at one sooner or later. A banquet is usually held in a restaurant, but there the resemblance to a restaurant dinner ends. At a banquet, you're in someone else's hands and you do what you're told.

A cocktail hour nearly always precedes dinner, which gives everyone a chance to gather together. "No-Host Bar" means you pay for your own drinks. An "Open Bar" provides free drinks. If you don't attend the cocktail reception, you probably won't be missed, but you should be on time for the dinner. Restaurant management sees to it that banquets begin on time.

Numerous, large round tables fill most banquet halls. Your place at one may be designated by a place-card (which you will have to search for) or you may have to find a seat of your own. If you don't know anyone, you want to cast your eye quickly around for people who at least look compatible, and then present yourself at that table and inquire if there is an empty chair. You will be expected to converse with your tablemates.

Sometimes the tablemates join in ordering bottles of wine, each person paying for a share. You will not have a choice of foods and don't expect any personal service. The group rate the organisation is paying for the dinner is based on efficiency. Servers are capable of sweeping the meal on and off very quickly and hope you will not linger too long over your plate. The speech-making usually begins as soon as the coffee has come around, and any further clanking of cups and spoons should be subdued. Banquet speakers are generally forced to contain their remarks within strict time guidelines, but the social hour may go on after the meeting has officially adjourned.

If you are the honoured guest, you will probably sit at the head table and not have to pay for your drinks. If you make a speech and people applaud, don't applaud back. You would then appear to be clapping for yourself. Just look gracious, allow a small smile to upturn your lips, and nod your head in acknowledgement.

GIFTS

Giving

Except for a few special occasions, Americans are not big gift-givers. Although a salesman may pass out free samples, there is no ritual exchange of presents among executives. In fact, if one American businessman were to give another a nicely wrapped present that had no bearing on the company's business, the recipient would consider the gift quite inexplicable, unless the object were valuable. Then the move could look like an embarrassing attempt at bribery. Even an inexpensive present could be taken as a slightly crass attempt to win somebody's consideration.

Americans have learned something of the role that gift-giving plays in certain other cultures, and when an American businessman goes to Tokyo, he goes equipped. But among ourselves, we don't see that we need presents. Presents cement the blossoming friendship among business partners, but as we don't need friendship to do business, we don't need presents either. We have contracts instead.

Even friends may never exchange presents. When I go abroad, I try to bring back little mementoes for close friends, but nobody would feel slighted if I didn't. I may occasionally buy a copy of a book for a friend, but I rarely remember a friend's birthday, and few people outside of family remember mine. If someone gave me presents too often I would think it tiresome, and I would feel the burden of having to reciprocate. Besides, like most Americans, I have plenty of stuff already.

However, a gift from a foreigner – suitably typical of his or her homeland – has greater dimensions than anything my fellow American could give me and won't go wrong, except to government employees who are prohibited from accepting gifts. Otherwise, don't hesitate to give small tokens to personal or business friends if you want to. But don't be insulted if you get nothing in exchange.

Receiving

One usually opens a present immediately and in front of the donor. (Exceptions: Christmas and birthday presents may be saved for the day, and wedding presents, as mentioned, are not opened at the wedding.) The best reaction is outright pleasure and delight at receiving something so lovely/indispensable/thoughtful. Show as much enthusiasm as possible and return to the subject periodically thereafter.

The donor will be particularly pleased if you emphasise that the gift shows his or her unusual sensitivity to you and your tastes. ("How did you know that my old sugar bowl broke and that I collect Scottish china'?" or "Peonies are my favorite flowers!") It is not necessary to go on much about how the donor shouldn't have gone to all the trouble, etc. Too much of that and we begin to think maybe indeed we shouldn't have and become embarrassed that we did.

The Guest

You may want to bring a bottle of wine or flowers to a dinner party, but the practice varies in different social sets and you are never expected to. In more formal houses, the flowers may already be magnificently arranged, and your hosts do not at the moment of your arrival wish to go poking around looking for the right vase. Nobody will mind if you bring a nice wine, but your host is not obliged to serve it that evening. The grander the house, the less appropriate a present is. After all, you wouldn't show up at the White House with a bottle of wine under your arm.

It is customary (although not obligatory) to bring something if you are going to be an overnight guest in someone's house. Some gourmet item, a good cheese, a present for the children – any little thing that shows your appreciation. It needn't be wrapped. You might instead send a gift afterwards.

Christmas

Christmas accounts for most of the necessary gift-giving in this country. Children in many families receive presents only at Christmas and on their birthdays – but then frequently in great quantity. Some people give all their relatives presents; others only give to their immediate family. Children are expected to give as well as to get presents.

Some friends exchange presents at Christmas and some don't. Some instead give presents to the small children of friends. I usually keep a few spare presents on hand around Christmas of the generic type – candles, fruitcake – wrapped under the Christmas tree so that if people unexpectedly produce presents for me, I have something for them.

Christmas is the time to settle the score with anyone who has been helpful throughout the year. There are certain required cash outlays – to doormen, babysitters, house cleaners, newspaper deliverers – for anyone who has served you regularly (*see* "Tipping" *in the Appendix for details*). You might want to give a little something (not money!) to your children's teachers or to those among them who have especially extended themselves.

There is a considerable flow of liquor bottles during the holiday season. In business, Christmas presents are often a one-way street where the buyer gets the present. If a company has been favoring you with their business, you give. They don't need to give you anything; it's enough that they pay their bills.

Within the company, bosses may hand around gifts to their subordinates – or they may not. Many companies give a small Christmas bonus to all personnel. A hard-working secretary is often rewarded with something rather nice, and if the secretary is particularly fond of his or her boss, the boss may get a present too. It is unlikely that you need to provide presents for all your co-workers, though if you work in a small group, everyone may give each other presents. Some departments have lotteries; a hat goes around with everyone's name in it, and you bring a small present to the Christmas party for the person whose name you drew.

Chapter Eleven

THE AMERICAN WOMAN

Just how liberated are American women? In theory, we are the equals of men in every way. Many foreigners think that American women are on top of the world. But in fact, any number of studies show that women, no matter how brilliant, are not taken as seriously as men. Furthermore, the average woman earns 76 cents for every dollar a man makes and does most of the housework too.

As a nation, however, we are committed to the equal rights of women. Jokes about women – as weak, flighty, bad drivers, extravagant, etc. – are considered tasteless. In the legal realm, there has been an enormous surge towards equality in the last 30 years. Employers who do not promote women now may get sued. The "Help Wanted" ads in newspapers used to be divided into columns for men and women, with clerical jobs for the women and managerial ones for the men. Now, a woman can aspire to nearly any job or training program. Women doctors, lawyers, and engineers are far more common than they were a few decades ago.

There are still not nearly as many women as men in the top ranks. A woman is a rare bird in the executive room of a corporation. But an increasing number of women have moved to top government jobs, and the idea of a woman president of the USA is not inconceivable.

It is not solely discrimination that holds women back. Women remain accountable for the children, and the total commitment required for a high-powered career makes it very difficult to be a satisfactory mother too. Sixty percent of top executive women have no children.

Superwomen

The "Superwoman Syndrome" refers to the efforts of women to excel as worker, wife, and mother. The well-paid working mother can provide nannies as substitutes for herself, but she may not escape the guilt that comes from not spending more time with her children. The conclusion is always that no one can be Superwoman, although some women give it a jolly good try.

Even the ordinary working woman leads a life of ceaseless motion. She rises early, sees children off to school, and races out of the house to her job. She may commute a long way to work, perhaps dropping off a child on the way. Coming home, she picks up children, then does errands, cooks dinner, supervises play and homework, puts children to bed, and prepares herself for another day's work.

The average woman also feels the obligation to remain attractive and youthful, which requires hours devoted to exercise, beauticians, make-up, and shopping. The American woman often seems (or at least feels) less self-confident than her counterparts from other lands.

She has spent an inordinate amount of her girlhood and her youth worrying about how to attract men, and her efforts have left her less natural than she might be otherwise. In *Lost in Translation,* Eva Hoffman writes of the time and effort American girls expend on femininity. She herself, a Pole, "never thought you had to do anything special to be feminine – surely, it's enough to be a woman, isn't it?" Not in the American woman's mind, which is much affected by advertising.

When the women's liberation movement accelerated in the seventies, feminists hoped that the good female values would change the world for the better – businesses would become less competitive and more concerned with humane values, men would joyfully take on their share of child-rearing, and women would no longer need to struggle to look like Marilyn Monroe. But on the contrary, women have instead moulded themselves to fit into what is still regarded as "a man's world." While women's dress is more varied than men's, they must bring the same hardheaded attitude to business to succeed.

The Foreign Man/The American Woman

To foreigners, American women may appear extremely free. The fact that American men help at all with housework shocks some. But the man who folds laundry and makes beds is not losing his manhood. When an American man goes out to find a wife, he is looking for a partner – someone with mutual interests, interesting conversation, an earning capacity, and a sense of humor. He can hardly expect his wife to be equal on most scores and inferior when it comes to washing the kitchen floor.

If you are a man from a country where women don't enter into men's territory, you may need to make an effort to treat women as equals. This means not asking the woman of the house about the children and then turning to the husband and saying, "And what do you think of the Mideast situation?" Women think about these things too. You could find rewarding new realms of conversation opening to you.

Certainly you would not whistle at a woman, make lewd remarks, or try to hustle any stray woman off to bed.

A woman traveling alone, eating in a restaurant alone, or doing anything else alone may be very satisfied with her own company and not welcome intrusion (although she may be open to a tactful approach). She will certainly find very annoying any assumption that she is pining for a man.

Almost half of American women are now single, and a quarter of those have never married. Many of these have discovered that they prefer not to marry. A single American woman has no obligation to stay home and look after aging parents and other people's children. Instead, she may have a wonderful career and an interesting life and count herself luckier than her married friends. One of the main disadvantages of being single is the idea that such a woman must be a loser. Surveys and statistics of health and happiness prove that on average, compared to the married woman, she isn't.

— *Chapter Twelve* —

THE AMERICAN HOME

Let us take a little tour of a typical American home, a middle class, middle-priced one in an average suburb. For all the differences among Americans, many such houses across the country are remarkably alike.

We will arrive by car because there is no other way. As there is so little demand for one, no public bus comes down this street. Most of the families in this neighbourhood have two cars, and a school bus may pick up the children.

The house we will visit is a one-storey "ranch" house built in the 1970s. We park directly in front, step out onto the sidewalk, and lock our car. It is midday, and there are no signs of people anywhere. Few people ever walk around here; there are no stores, restaurants, or bars within walking distance. If any of the neighbors were in their front yards, we would see them because there are few fences around the yards. A few shrubs separate one piece of property from another.

We walk up the front path. On either side of us is an expanse of green lawn, usually maintained by the man of the house or by a garden service. This lawn is part of the great lawn that spreads across America, cultivated on deserts, mountains, and seashores – a triumph over the wilderness. Few crops are more unnatural or more difficult to grow than a velvety green lawn, which must be planted, weeded, fertilized, watered, and cut regularly. By our lawns are we judged. Your neighbor may know nothing about you, but he will note the condition of your lawn.

Photo: Esther Wanning

This typical American ranch home could be found anywhere in the USA.

203

THE AMERICAN HOME

We push a button by the door and hear a ding-dong chiming inside. Very quickly someone answers. It is our host. Our hostess comes to greet us at the door as well. "Let's not stand around in the hall," she says. "Do come in." We follow the beige wall-to-wall carpeting into the living room, which is sparsely decorated with two white couches and several white easy chairs.

"Sit down and make yourselves comfortable," says our host. There are large color photographs of the children, framed in silver, on the walls, along with some framed museum posters. A glass coffee table has a copy of an immense book on it, *The Art of the Vatican*. There are no other books in this room. There are copies of *Time, Martha Stewart's Living, Money Magazine* and *TV Guide* on the coffee table. A large unit on one wall encases a television, a DVD player, and a stereo.

The front curtains are always drawn because our hosts do not like the idea that someone walking by their house could see into their living room. However, the large side windows of the room let light stream in.

Electricity

We are served coffee, made in an electric coffeepot. Our hostess takes some chocolate chip cookies from the freezer and thaws them by putting them in the microwave oven for a minute. The electricity supply is very good and steady; there is rarely a power outage. Power lines are often buried underground so you may not see any power poles outside.

If there were a power outage, these household essentials would stop working: the refrigerator, the freezer, the microwave oven, the clock radio, the televisions and stereo, the computer, the telephone answering machine, the cell phone recharger, the doorbell, the garage door opener, the dishwasher, the clothes washer and dryer, the lights, the food processor, the electric blender, the bread maker, the electric toothbrush, and the air-conditioner. The burglar alarm has a battery backup so a thief cannot disconnect it by cutting the electrical wires to the house.

Climate Control

On hot days, the family closes the windows and doors and turns on the central air-conditioner. Cold air circulates throughout the house. Less modern houses have window air-conditioners, which only cool one room apiece. Some old houses and apartment buildings do not have adequate wiring to run air-conditioners, and a few people don't like them anyhow because of their noise and the artificial chill they produce. In the summer, open windows have screens in them, which keep flies and mosquitoes out.

In the winter, the central heating in this house can be counted on to heat all the rooms equally. In cold areas, storm windows are put up in the fall for insulation. The furnace is in the basement and vents in each room distribute the heat. Not driven together to heat themselves by a stove, family members may spend much of their time in the privacy of their own rooms.

House Tour

Foreigners often think it strange that Americans will show them every room of the house. "No wonder they don't want people dropping in," says an Irish woman, "when it means cleaning the entire house." But our hosts expect that we are curious to see everything, and they are rather proud of the size and decor of the bedrooms and of the pretty wallpaper in the bathrooms.

The dining room is an extension of the living room. We walk through it to see the kitchen, which is big and airy and sparkling clean. The appliances are all a matching cream color and look new. The refrigerator is six feet tall, defrosts itself, and produces ice cubes and ice water automatically. The kitchen has a glass door to the large back yard, which has a jungle gym in it that the children used when they were small. There is no swimming pool. This isn't Hollywood.

The other wing of the house has three bedrooms. As each of the two children has a room, and the parents the third, there is no guest room or study. But guests can sleep on one of the living room couches, which opens into a bed.

Each of the children's rooms is crammed with things: toys, games, a desk, a computer in one and a stereo in the other, stuffed animals, an encyclopedia, big posters of rock stars on the walls, a bookcase full of books. The older child has a telephone with her own phone line. There are in all four telephones in this house. Each family member also has a cell phone so that they can always locate each other.

The parents' room is large, with a king-size bed and its own bathroom. There is another bathroom off the hallway, and each bathroom has a sink, toilet, and bathtub with shower. There are no bidets. The bathrooms are tiled and have pretty matching towels on the racks. If this were a newer, more luxurious house there would be even more bathrooms and perhaps a hot tub and jacuzzi (a large tub with swirling water) in the backyard.

There is no drain on the bathroom floor, and people who are bathing try not to splash. There's a bath-mat folded on the side of a tub, which you put on the floor when you're taking a bath. You fill the tub, wash and relax, then get out carefully and stand drying yourself on the bath-mat. When you take a shower, you close the shower curtain, keeping its bottom side inside the tub to keep the water in. When you're finished, you turn the water off.

There are many different kinds of faucets in use, and you may have to ask how to use them. The ones in showers can be especially tricky. When you're turning the water off, don't use excessive force or you may break the faucet.

A bathroom door is often closed even when nobody is inside, so you must knock before entering. Whether or not a man should leave the toilet seat up or down is a subject of debate in American homes. If you're wondering, leave it down.

Our final stop is the garage, where our host has his workshop. Far from being ashamed of manual labor, Americans take pride in being able to fix and make things. A man in particular likes to be "handy," and our host fixes broken chairs, changes electrical cords, and refinishes worn furniture at his workbench. Along the wall, there are shelves of leftover paint. The lady of the house has painted all the walls herself.

Not for the Ages

We think we could be comfortable here in this spacious, quiet house – at least for a while. It seems very anonymous, having been built from the same plans from which thousands of other houses across America were built. There was no attempt to make the house suit the landscape or the climate. The walls are not thick and sturdy; the doors are hollow. There is no wood trim or extra decor, the closets are small, and the ceilings are low. There is no fireplace. To many Europeans, these suburban houses are not well built. The people who occupy them do not think of living in one place all their lives. They certainly don't expect that their children will grow up and stay in the same place. When people plan improvements, they often think more about what will increase the resale value than of what they themselves would most like.

Inside, there are no hidden nooks and crannies, no secret places, no signs of wear. The furniture is new; there are no family heirlooms and little that indicates the personalities of the occupants, despite their many interests. The house is so tidy that evidence of their hobbies is all hidden away.

Americans are consumers, not collectors. What happens to all the stuff they buy? Drive around on a Saturday or a Sunday and you will find garage sales. The family puts prices on their excess goods and sets them out in front of the garage. Everything from shoes that pinched to the old couch can be found for sale in a festive atmosphere, and if you like to bargain, this is your chance. Garage sales are a reasonable way for newcomers to furnish their houses. (You might also want to investigate resale shops, to which some people donate their used goods, if you're trying to set up housekeeping cheaply.) The stuff that people don't want to use or get rid of may be down in their basements, up in their attics, or in storage. Storage units rent for $50/month and up, and a surprising number of people spend large amounts of money to keep things that they readily admit are junk.

Household Helpers

We rarely use the term "servants," a word that offends our ideas of democracy. They are house cleaners or housekeepers or babysitters or cooks – terms that imply some specialty other than being subservient.

American women have been lamenting the household help problem for generations, although there used to be a supply of immigrants or African-American women to do other people's housework. Then in World War II, the household helpers went off to work in the factories and afterwards never wanted to work in other ladies' houses again. And no wonder – the pay is bad, the employer can be difficult, and there are few benefits.

Most families are now accustomed to doing most of the household work themselves. Because so often both adults have jobs outside the home, professional families often have house cleaners who come in one or more times a week to do the general cleaning. But only very wealthy people still have cooks, gardeners, and daily housekeepers.

Consequently, families have found many short-cuts to make up for the fact that there is so often no mother who spends her day looking after the household. Breakfast may be a bowl of cereal, no one comes home for lunch, and dinner is often pizza or Chinese take-out food. There are numerous time-saving services, from plumbers who come in the evening to mail-order catalogues. Clothes are made of drip-dry fabrics or are sent to the dry-cleaners.

Americans are mad for time-saving devices, no matter how minuscule the time saved. Automatic-dial telephones, microwave-ready meals, automatic watering systems, power mowers, and electric garden clippers all give Americans the illusion that they may someday get time under control.

Nonetheless, the real work remains. The weekend for the typical hard-working family consists of shopping, cleaning, fixing things around the house, gardening, and an overall attempt to get ready for the next frantic week. Few people socialize much. Besides the various reasons taken up in chapters 9 and 10, there just isn't time.

Chapter Thirteen

DOING BUSINESS IN AMERICA

"The business of America is business," said President Calvin Coolidge in 1927. That statement is even more true today. Of all the ways to occupy one's time, work is the most important. Elsewhere, the sickness of a grandmother or the problems of a cousin would be reasonable excuses for taking a day off. Not so here. Nearly every other element of life is sacrificed before the work part.

Foreigners generally surmise that it's because "the dollar is king" that Americans are so work-crazy and that the unabashed fever for moneymaking overrides the finer feelings. There's some truth to this, but there's more than money driving the worker.

The Value of Work

A belief in progress, a sense of infinite resources, and an emphasis on tangible results contribute to unbounded enthusiasm for undertaking new projects. As an American's self-image is dependent on action, even personal wealth does not inhibit the work ethic.

To work well and hard is a high value. Although there are many who do neither, they are not the people who win the admiration of their peers, nor the ones who rise to the top. Those who want to command respect apply themselves diligently. No matter how splendid someone might be on other fronts, she does not wish to be thought remiss as a worker. Better to be labeled a bad daughter or thoughtless friend. Self-esteem is bound up in achievement, and when people lose their jobs or retire they often become depressed, even when money is not a problem. The more successful the person, the more likely it is that his life revolves around his or her career rather than around home and family.

A degree of unfettered ambition, one that might even be found unattractive in other countries, is admired here. An Englishman would not care to be known as "all business." An American would. At the bottom of the career ladder, where people serve fast food for minimum wage, people work hard, but the job does not overlap into leisure hours. The higher one rises, the more all-consuming the job becomes.

Company Operations: The Bottom Line

The company is in business for one reason: to make a profit for the owners – individuals or stockholders – and to make more profit than could be made if the capital were invested otherwise. This is not simple as many businesses are up against cutthroat competition and must keep prices low or lose market share.

This single-minded dedication to profits leads to ruthless operations. American companies are quick to throw out the old and bring in the new. Typically, they make only short-range plans and want fast profits. Since the eighties, when the USA became the world's biggest debtor nation, more and more companies have felt under attack. Publicly held companies are subject to unfriendly takeovers. Most companies do not feel stable enough to make their workers too comfortable, and job security is not a feature of American worklife.

The Enron and WorldCom scandals and bankruptcies revealed the extent to which some companies will go to succeed. However, these companies went way beyond usual procedures and were not typical of US business. You are unlikely to be asked to engage in shady operations in US companies. But you may find your company's policies rather heartless.

In countries such as Japan, social benefits are part of national and corporate philosophy; companies factor in the higher costs of keeping everyone employed and using goods made at home, etc. The extra costs are paid for through higher consumer prices. The American viewpoint is that the citizen/consumer, who is also the worker, is best served by the lowest prices. In the process, workers may lose their jobs but the deserving will find other ones. Thus by an "invisible hand," the economy is directed to function in the most efficient manner – at a cost of much upheaval and dislocation.

The Job Hop

As companies are constantly reorganizing, retrenching, and being bought and sold, they have many occasions to lay off workers. They may do so regretfully, but they feel no compulsion to go on supporting the unprofitable employee. Companies have been so ruthlessly "downsizing" for the last couple of decades that it seems that every remaining employee is doing the work of two or three people. Those who do have jobs live in fear of losing them, and when the axe does fall, people are usually asked to clear out their desks quickly.

The workers on their side are always free to improve their situations by looking out for new jobs. In fact, this is about the only right an individual (unless a member of a union, as are only 13.5% of

American workers) has in a corporation. So workers are quick to move if a better opportunity presents itself. Were company fidelity alone to cause someone to reject brighter prospects, her colleagues would probably think him or her stupid. After all, someone who doesn't move voluntarily may end up moving involuntarily.

However, options are limited for job seekers. Many manufacturing jobs have been lost in the past decades, so blue-collar (manual) workers especially have limited options. Many of the newly created jobs in our economy are in the service sector and poorly paid. The federally mandated minimum wage has been stuck at $5.15 an hour (at this writing) for the past seven years, and a raise is overdue. A minimum-wage worker is now worse off than he was thirty years ago. White-collar workers may make decent salaries and even receive benefits, but downsizing, mergers, and market fluctuations keep everyone hopping.

Executives

Life at the top is very different from life at the bottom, except in one regard – it can be just as insecure. Mistakes are not easily forgiven, and even a long-time employee in the highest ranks can be summarily dismissed. (Those at the top, however, will probably leave with a very handsome severance package, whereas lower down, a few weeks pay may be the most the worker can hope for.) Those closely associated with the ousted executive may be out the door as well, leading to Byzantine politics in which underlings try to keep lines of communication open to several factions within the company.

Democracy has little place in the American corporation. Important decisions are made at the top, usually in secrecy, and based on a heavy weight of facts and figures. The chief executive officer may take complete responsibility for a key decision after thrashing it out in executive meetings.

As few people are involved, a decision in the USA can be made quickly. However, it may take longer to implement than in a system in which everyone was involved beforehand in making the decision. If a venture goes bad, the person who championed it can be fired, which would not occur where there is consensus management. The person fired could be the chief executive officer.

Business life is tense. Few American companies can stand still and reap the rewards of America's one-time advantages. The playing field has levelled and foreign companies are successfully competing. It's a rare executive who is in a position to relax.

Executive Life

For his trouble, the fellow (it almost certainly is a man) at the top is extremely well compensated. The differential between top and bottom salaries in the USA is extraordinary, and even in companies doing badly, chief executives collect millions of dollars a year in pay, stock options, and bonuses. Those at the very top take home 400 times as much as the average worker. Furthermore, while executive remuneration has soared, taxes in the highest income bracket have come down. Millionaires are now commonplace.

Amiability is not a prerequisite for rising to the top, and there are a number of chief executive officers with legendary bad tempers. It is not the boss's job to worry about the wellbeing of his subordinates (although the man with many enemies will be swept out more quickly in hard times); it's the company he worries about. His business savvy is supposed to be based on intimate knowledge of his company and the industry so he goes home nightly with a full briefcase. At the very top – and on the way up – executives are exceedingly dedicated.

The American executive must be capable of enough small talk to get him through the social part of his schedule, but he is probably not a highly cultured individual or an intellectual. Although his wife may be on the board of the symphony or opera, he himself has little time for such pursuits. His reading may largely concern business and management (American companies are often trendy in their attempts to keep up with the latest innovations in business methods), despite interests in other fields. Golf provides him with a sportive outlet that combines with some useful business socializing.

These days, he probably attempts some form of aerobic exercise to "keep the old heart in shape" and for the same reason goes easy on butter and alcohol, substances thought to contribute to taking highly stressed executives out of the running. (These health endeavors may be favorite conversational subjects.) But his doctor's admonition to "take it easy" falls on deaf ears. He likes to work. He knows there are younger men nipping at his heels. Despite the occasional newspaper article about the executive who gives up the rat race, few actually are eager to be put out to pasture.

They may, however, be quite willing to move on to greener pastures. Corporate head-hunting, carried on by "executive search firms," is a growth industry. America has great faith in individual talent, and dynamic, aggressive executives are so in demand that companies regularly raid each other's managerial ranks.

Employee Life

"In Argentina I worked just as hard," an Argentinian architect complained, "but work wasn't as stressful or competitive as it is in the USA. There you feel part of a group that helps each other, but here you feel disposable."

Foreign employees of American companies sometimes feel the lack of spoken praise, which is often felt to be superfluous here. Good work is noted and rewarded with salary increases and promotions or in these days of stagnant salaries, it simply may not be noted at all. Bad work is usually quickly brought to the employee's attention.

Competitive tension here goads the workers on, but it also causes a high level of anxiety. Individual effort prevails over teamwork. When results are quantifiable, many companies give awards to the most productive workers, thus pitting one worker against another. If a decision is made because one person's point of view prevailed, that person is held responsible for the outcome and will get the credit if the idea succeeds – no matter how many people helped implement it. If the idea fails, the person will also shoulder the blame. While there's always some give and take among people who work together, the level of trust in an office may be low.

Company loyalty is also rather slight, and people identify themselves by their job ("I am a bank manager") rather than by company name. Co-workers may speak very derisively of the company among themselves ("Thank God it's Friday and I'm outa here"), although it's understood that this doesn't affect the quality of their efforts. Within the company, while one might have some loyalty to one's manager, one would not be expected to put one's own job on the line for him or her. It is to yourself that you are expected to be true.

Despite the stress level, many foreigners find the American work climate very satisfying, particularly ambitious people who felt stymied in their own cultures. "America is the best place for work," says an English woman, now staying home with her baby. "Working so hard was very stimulating, and I found my job exciting and rewarding." Even many of those who complain about the relentlessness of the pace admit they would be bored in a more restful atmosphere.

Hiring

The process of interviewing and hiring for job vacancies usually is an even-handed one. If no one is on the spot for an opening, the company advertises it in the newspaper (which you nearly always can access online), posts it on a web site such as www.craigslist.org, or lists it with an employment agency. Resumes roll in, and the candidates with the most promising records are invited in for interviews and get a chance to demonstrate ease of manner, enthusiasm, experience, and ideas. This is not the moment for undue modesty (although one should not sound like an unbearable braggart). There are many books of advice for the job seeker, and the newcomer to America would be wise to consult the literature. By law, women and minority applicants must be given equal consideration.

Although connections are not necessary even for the best jobs, the person who comes recommended has an edge. However, in the end, nobody will hire you just because you are so-and-so's niece or nephew. Even if you are, your qualifications will have to be at least as good as the competition's. In some cases, a relationship could be a drawback as nepotism is looked on unfavorably. The main thing a company is usually looking for is somebody who has done exactly the same sort of work before.

Despite the opinion of many business journalists that the MBA's (persons holding degrees in business administration) are wrecking American business with their narrow, methodical, cold-blooded methods, and although they are disdained by many old-line entrepreneurs, these MBA's are much in demand and those from the elite schools start with very high salaries.

Personnel Policies

Company employment policies are nearly all neatly codified and presented to the new employee at the time of hiring. Although a company has the fundamental right to dismiss an employee at any time, recent lawsuits have caused most companies to carefully document the procedure leading to firings.

Work hours, vacation time, breaks, pension plans, sick leave, and rights are itemized and administered with impartiality. No matter if one person has a dying mother, and another develops disabilities. Mitigating factors may be tolerated for a time, but the employee who can't meet the standards can expect eventually to be dismissed.

There are, of course, exceptions to the impersonal approach and many cases of companies that have stuck by their workers through thick and thin. But even then, the bosses will probably excuse themselves by saying, "She was too good a worker to lose. We knew she'd be back some day." Whether true or not, nobody would want to admit that a business decision had been tilted by purely human considerations.

217

Photo: Kristy MacDonald

Department meetings can be very informal.

Office Relationships

Most offices are informal, with lots of joking around, back-slapping, and breeziness. Office doors are usually left open, unless a meeting is in progress. Although everybody knows perfectly well who the boss is – and subtly jockey for attention – the deference paid is less obvious than in more hierarchical societies.

For many people, the workplace becomes a substitute for the community that is fast disappearing from urban life. It's in the office that gossip, recipes, and names of barbers are exchanged and where someone will listen to how your date went last night. The department will take you out to lunch on your birthday and send you flowers when you're bereaved. The young and single may drink together, rent ski cabins in the winter, and set up blind dates for each other.

Nonetheless, it's a transitory community. Few groups stay intact for long. The members bond together for a while, but the ties are fragile and often don't outlast a regrouping. Americans are good at the quick relationship – thick today, gone tomorrow. After all, in the course of a career, a vast number of paths cross, and it would be impossible to keep up with all of them.

Managers do not routinely involve themselves in their subordinates' personal lives. They may indulge in some friendly chat on personal subjects, but they do not consider themselves responsible for anyone's emotional wellbeing. This is not pure hardboiled indifference but reflects also the respect for privacy which so often in American life takes primacy over other needs. The American viewpoint is that the worker has a right to conduct his personal life however he sees fit as long as it does not affect his job performance. Despite the separation of job and life, many workers keep pictures of wives, husbands, children and dogs on their desks, a practice some foreigners find very odd.

Initiative Before Deference
The hierarchy is not rigid in most offices. Managers encourage ideas from subordinates, and subordinates may contradict their superiors. Promotion is by no means orderly, and tomorrow you may be reporting to someone who reported to you yesterday.

It doesn't hurt to be pushy and aggressive (within reason). The theory is that if you're aggressive in your own cause, you'll exert yourself for the company too. You can get away with stepping on a few toes on the way up, although it's wise to cultivate supporters as well.

One large California computer company runs a special course for its Asian-born employees, a course popularly known as "rudeness training." The intent is to teach those from non-confrontational cultures how to be direct and assertive towards clients, co-workers, and to their own bosses.

Corporate Cultures
In stereotype at least, office atmosphere varies from coast to coast. New York is frenetic, pressured, and more formal than elsewhere; the

Midwest is conventional and methodical; the West Coast allows a degree of nonconformity. But you can also expect to find laid-back offices in New York and formal ones in Los Angeles. Even in Midwestern Chicago, you'll come across eccentricity.

Beyond locale, particular companies are known for distinctive "corporate cultures." There are those that pride themselves on creating a family atmosphere and provide employees with unusual security. Many companies run bowling leagues and baseball teams, and on weekends the employees' children paddle in the company pool. (But even some of these old-style companies, such as IBM, have been laying off large numbers of workers lately.)

Some companies make a point of giving employees an enormous amount of autonomy ("We don't care what you do or how you do it, just get results".) There are companies that emphasise creativity, and others that are very disciplined; some have rigid chains of command and others almost imperceptible chains. Many, goaded on by those books and courses on management, are constantly dreaming up new ways of organising and issuing new work flow charts.

The human factor may anywhere override a particular company's stance. The manager of one department in a company may develop strong team spirit, whereas another whips up a deadly competition. In the end, however, both managers must produce results.

DOING BUSINESS WITH AMERICANS

Get to the Point

By all reports, the single greatest difference between business dealings in the USA and the rest of the world is the American eagerness to get to the point. Most peoples of the world don't negotiate with strangers. Therefore the first order of business is to get to know their callers, no matter how long it takes. Then they can decide if these are people they want to work with.

All this is a mystery to an American. Why sit around jawing and drinking cup after cup of coffee when you could be making deals? Certainly we want to know if you can deliver, the strength of your company, your resources. Why don't you tell us that instead of about the beauty of Tang Dynasty vases? Then we can get down to how much, when, and who pays for what. At the end of several days when the American realizes that he and his new friends haven't yet lighted on one significant aspect of the business he came to talk about, he's ready to exit by the nearest window.

It's not that we're automatons. We're friendly, and we want to be liked. We're glad to have a little let's-all-relax chitchat at the beginning of a meeting. We'll even occasionally offer you coffee, if the company coffeepot isn't too far away. We'll take you out to lunch, but by the main course we expect to have the pleasantries out of the way and get down to brass tacks. We just don't think it's necessary to know someone very well to do business with them. After all, if we find we don't like you after we've done a little business, we can dump your company and try a different one.

Another reason that we want to get on with the business at hand is that it's what interests us. Whereas business people from other countries may be frankly bored with business and prefer to talk about other things, Americans are not. It's abstract conversations that bore us; the pragmatic American likes a conversation that is going somewhere. Stuck making small talk for hours, we're like racehorses shut up in the paddock. We long for a chance to show our stuff.

Tick Tock

In the mind of the American business person the clock is always ticking, and there are further worlds to conquer. Why spend any more time than necessary on this deal? We feel no need to be soulmates. We are not going to base this relationship on trust anyhow. We are going to base it on an elaborate, detailed contract which our lawyers will draw up.

During the workday, Americans are very precise about time. If you're ten minutes late for an appointment, you should apologize. If you're half an hour late, you should have a good reason. When you see your American host drumming his fingers and looking at his watch, wrap up the meeting quickly. And don't be insulted if he announces he has another meeting and unceremoniously turns you out of his office. Very likely he does have another meeting, and even if you're in the middle of a critical conversation, he has to be there on time. It doesn't mean that he's any less interested in your business.

Making Contact

As anywhere, when you're trying to get in the door it helps to have mutual acquaintances. But if you don't, the formal approach is perfectly acceptable. Find out who is in charge of the area of your interest and write a letter, in English, typed, stating your credentials, intentions, and email address. You may want to open negotiations at the top, by having your president contact the American company's president.

If you don't get a reply, follow up with another letter or a phone call. It's helpful to have an exchange of correspondence before you arrive for a meeting so the Americans can consider your proposal and involve the right people.

If you're flying in for a meeting, be sure you have an appointment before you arrive. Americans keep tightly packed schedules, and should you arrive without appointments, you could discover that your important contacts have absolutely no time to see you – no matter how important you are.

Meetings

A lot of business decisions are made in meetings, which can be stormy. Those in attendance are expected to bring up objections, thrash out problems, and defend their positions. Those in a losing position are not supposed to brood about loss of face.

To many foreigners, the American approach is cold and rational; we like a proposal that is based on facts and figures. Of course, we want to know that you're reliable, but our main interest is price, and we are incredulous to hear that in some cultures the business relationship is more important than the price.

Americans will appreciate it if you show up at a meeting armed with all the pertinent statistics and deliver a well-rounded pitch, including the data that proves what a great company you represent. It's a good idea to work in how great you are too, although you must be a little more offhand in forwarding yourself. Americans accept arrogance, but too much boasting can arouse doubts. "Doing business is completely different here," says a Japanese businessman. "I make my presentation, they ask questions and I'm done."

We favor fast-talking, smooth operators, which is why some of our most sparkling representatives fail in countries where fast talkers are distrusted. Humility goes a lot further outside the United States. The important thing here is to make it clear that you are a "can-do" kind of person and that you understand what the Americans want.

Straightforwardness

Americans do not appreciate being "strung along." If, as is done in some countries, you offer pleasant reassurances that turn out not to be true, American business people will be highly annoyed – "Why the devil didn't someone tell us?" We want the straight scoop, the real story. If you can't deliver when you said you would (and June 1 means June 1, not sometime in June) tell us now so we can plan for it. We'll still like you better than the bunch who couldn't deliver and didn't tell us about it.

Those from the Far East may be shocked by the bluntness with which an American reports negative news. "Sorry, but we got a better price from someone else," or "Those blouses were badly made." In another culture your feelings would be considered more important than the truth, whereas we consider that we're doing you a favor by our straightforwardness. Now you know why you're not getting our business and can do something about it. And we've saved you from wasting your time in anticipation. But this can seem very cold-hearted and rude in some cultures.

Accountability

You may find the decision-making process fairly streamlined in an American company, compared to that in other countries. Certain key decisions will probably require an executive board's approval, but very often there are somebodies along the line with the authority to make lesser decisions. Who these people are is generally not a secret.

Business Entertaining

Americans can be lavish entertainers. We see the value in breaking bread with our counterparts from other countries and most executives have quite decent expense accounts. But few would care to be out every night. If you find yourself less royally entertained than in some other countries, it could be because most Americans prefer a steak and salad themselves to what they regard as the tedium of a five-course meal in a French restaurant.

As conversation isn't our favorite indulgence either, we assume that you too would be as glad to lie down and take off your shoes as to be dragged all over town. So a night out with American hosts will probably not be excessively long. Americans do not consider that their manhood requires them to sacrifice sleep.

If you are traveling with your spouse, be sure that your host knows it so that he or she won't be left out of evening plans. If the American wives (or husbands) don't appear, it is probably because they have business of their own, live in a distant suburb to which your host will be returning on the late night train, can't find a babysitter, or are bored stiff by business dinners.

Breakfast and Lunch

You may find yourself facing the business breakfast, favored by Americans who don't want to break up the business day, or who don't have enough lunches on their calendars to go around. If the thought of bacon and eggs at eight in the morning makes you sick, just have a roll and coffee. The point of the business breakfast is not to eat breakfast.

Lunches don't often last for much over an hour. Americans have never had the tradition of the long midday repast, and the practice of having a few drinks with lunch is long gone. At breakfast and lunch, the Americans will expect to talk business for at least part of the time; dinner can turn out to be purely social, particularly if couples are involved.

The person who did the inviting does the paying. If your hosts took you out the first time, you may wish to reciprocate and invite them the next. The Zagat restaurant guides are fairly reliable and have editions for many major cities.

Names, Rank, and Titles

Nearly everybody these days is on a first-name basis. If you prefer some other form of address, say so. One Japanese man, who after twelve years here still can't get used to strangers calling him by his first name, gives out his last name by itself, which Americans think is his first name.

Titles don't matter much in the business world. It's important to know who the company president is, but you wouldn't call him "President Watson." If you're not using a first name, say Mr., Mrs., Miss, or Ms. (*See* "What Do I Call You?" *in Chapter Nine.*)

You do need to know who the important people are at the meeting or else you may find yourself addressing your remarks to the distinguished looking older man who turns out to be the company bookkeeper rather than to the awkward-looking kid who happens to be the chief executive officer. Try to listen carefully when the introductions go by. Of course, even in America, there's enough homage paid to the boss so that observers don't have to be too brilliant to figure out who counts.

Business Cards

Cards play a minor role in American business and may not come out until the end of a meeting. They are used mainly to pass on an address and phone number, not as credentials. Most people have them, however, and you should too, printed in English.

Dress

Unless very sure of themselves, gentlemen visitors will probably do best to wear the kind of conservative suits that Brooks Brothers and Paul Stuart are known for: grey or dark blue, understated and well made. Nothing should be polyester or shiny, and the cut should be classic and conservative. Subtle tweeds are fine; pinstripes must be very narrow, barely perceptible as stripes. In the summer, a cotton khaki suit will do, although if you have a little panache you might get away with wearing seersucker.

You're safest in a white or light blue shirt. Drip-dry is acceptable as long as the naked eye can't tell the difference. Colored shirts with white collars are too trendy. A tie cannot be flamboyant, and any bright colors should be discreet. The pattern should be small, as in little dots or vague stripes. Never wear jewellery.

Black wing-tip shoes are usually favored among conservative dressers, although loafers will probably not shock anyone. Belts should be black.

These guidelines are merely starting points. California computer types and Texas oilmen allow themselves remarkable liberties, and when you know with whom you're dealing you can adapt. However, the above wardrobe will establish you as safe and trustworthy anywhere.

Photo: Esther Wanning

For sophisticated businessmen, the rules of dress don't change much: subdued colours, nothing shiny, well-polished shoes.

Women are allowed more color and variations. Some executive women disdain suits in favor of colorful skirts or dresses (often worn with a jacket), but if you want to be entirely safe, a suit with a skirt, worn with a simple shell or a neck scarf, and minimal jewelery, will take you anywhere. Even a designer pantsuit could be a little unconventional in a few rarified circles. In the winter, boots are ideal footwear, and in summer, shoes with thick heels, rather than spikes, are preferable for anyone with much walking to do.

Gifts

Forget about graft. No respectable business greases palms. (Yes, there are occasional scandals involving the government, but they're far outside the norm.) An American who found that someone had left him a briefcase full of money would be struck dumb. Even gifts are unusual, except at Christmas.

Business Hours

The standard working day is 9 to 5, although for executives those are minimal work hours. On the West Coast, working hours are often 8 to 5, and anyone in the West doing much business with the East has to get an early start. West Coast stockbrokers are at work by 6 a.m. (when it's 9 a.m. on the New York Stock Exchange). Some cities with major traffic problems encourage flexible work hours ("flex-time") so that within one company some people might work from 7 a.m. to 3 p.m. and others 10 a.m. to 6 p.m.

Americans do try to keep their weekends for home and family. You might, however, be invited to someone's home on the weekend for a dinner, barbecue, or brunch.

Some urban dwellers have weekend homes in the country and leave early on Fridays to get to them. It is a very favored guest who is invited to the country home. If you are so honored, write a thank-you note to your hostess afterwards.

Vacations

American vacation time is extremely short compared to European and even many Asian allotments. It increases with length of employment; most people qualify for only a couple of weeks a year. Eventually, some may receive a month's vacation, but usually take a week here and a week there, being loath to leave their offices for a month at a time. Because of the children's school holidays, summer is the commonest time for a break.

Frequently (life speeds up in more and more ways), people make the most of long weekends rather than take substantial vacations. Supposedly, fear of what will happen in their absences causes many people to settle for four-day holidays – just long enough for the New Yorker to fly down to the Caribbean.

Communicating

Americans are expected to answer their mail (postal and email), and they'll expect you to answer yours. If you don't, you'll be thought unreliable. So even if you don't have an immediate answer, it's best to write and say so. Messages can be very brief.

The telephone is heavily used. Many, many questions that would call for a personal meeting in another country are resolved over the phone here. We can happily do business with people we have never met at all.

Assistants

Persons of importance have an assistant (sometimes still called a secretary) who takes care of their appointments and correspondence and who is a buffer between the person and those demanding to see him or her. It's helpful if the assistant likes you, and you should learn his or her name. Although the assistant probably doesn't influence major decisions, he or she can forward your cause in various ways, not the least of which is in putting your phone calls through.

Photo: Esther Wanning

The well-dressed businesswoman looks more feminine than she did a few years ago. Knee length is the current designer choice for hems, but you can get away with longer or shorter skirts.

Women in Business

Although women are still rare in executive boardrooms, they are fast on their way up the ladder. Half the managerial positions in corporate America are held by women, and chances are good that your visiting foreign team will be meeting women who are doing the same job they are.

Some foreigners are not used to negotiating with women, but they should try to acclimatize very quickly or risk badly antagonizing a prospective business partner. Be sure that you are not in the habit of assuming that all women are underlings.

The correct procedure is simple: treat a woman as you would a man. This does not mean that you can't discreetly help her on with her coat after a business lunch, but you should ask her the same questions you would a man and give the same regard to the answers.

Allow a woman to pick up the check under any circumstances when a man in her position would pay. Don't take over in restaurants if she invited you; she understands a wine list. Do not be overly solicitous of her safety – she' s used to going home alone in a cab. And do not, under any circumstances, make a pass at her unless you want to see your whole deal go up in a puff of smoke.

The truth is that it is tough for a woman in a man's world. One reason is that the one endeavor that society takes as seriously as "worker" is "mother," and the working mother constantly feels she is cheating either her job or her children. (The working father can be regretful he sees his children so little, but he isn't considered a bad father.) She will appreciate it if you don't make her job any harder for her. If working with women is a new experience for you, you may be pleased to discover what a pleasure it can be. Even in America, many women insist, to get ahead they must be twice as good as a man.

CULTURAL QUIZ

Here follow a few situations over which some foreign visitors have been known to stumble. What would you do?

SITUATION ONE

You are a man employed by a large company, and many of your co-workers are women. Where you come from, strong barriers separated men and women, and you find you really like the looseness between the sexes here. To show how much you like working with women, you:

A Touch them often, draping an arm around the ladies' shoulders, or taking hold of a hand or arm.

B Compliment the women constantly on their hair, clothes, and pretty smiles.

C Compliment your female colleagues on their good work.

Comments

Although a lot of contact is permissible between men and women in this society, the office is not a dating situation, and women should be treated professionally. Too much of *A* could get you in hot water; you could even face charges of sexual harassment. *B* will simply be found annoying. *C* will be pleasing to one and all.

SITUATION TWO

You want to have a telephone installed quickly at your new apartment. You should:

A Call the telephone company and accept the first appointment for installation that you're offered.

B Appear in person at the telephone company's offices and explain how important it is that you get a phone promptly.

C Find someone with connections to the phone company who can see that you go to the top of the list.

Comments

A is all you need to do. Most businesses serve their customers impartially on the basis of first-come, first-served. Your phone is likely to be installed within a week.

SITUATION THREE

A friend has invited you to dinner at a nice restaurant. You dine well, and at the end the waiter brings the check and puts it in the middle of the table. You expect your friend to pick up the check, but he (or she) doesn't. You wait, and the conversation grows slow, and still he (she) doesn't. You are getting very tired and are beginning to think that you're expected to pick up the check. What do you do?

A Grit your teeth and wait some more.

B Pick up the check and pay it.

C Pick up the check and say, "Shall we split it?"

Comments

C is the most reasonable course of action. You could also just produce your share of the check, based on what you ate and drank.

You may have been justified in expecting him to pay, particularly if he selected the restaurant. But people often propose meals together without intending to pay for the other person. If your friend happens to be a client of yours, he might be hoping you'll pay, but if the dinner was his idea he should not expect you to. Unless you're very sure someone is paying for you, take enough money to cover dinner when you go out.

SITUATION FOUR

In the college cafeteria, you meet an American and fall into a long and revealing conversation. You are new in the USA and lonely. Here, you think, is a real friend. You exchange phone numbers, but your new friend doesn't call. The following week, you see her again in the cafeteria, but although she smiles and says "hi" in a friendly way, she passes by your table to sit with other people. You feel very hurt. What has happened?

A She found out more about you and decided not to pursue the friendship.

B Much as she enjoyed the conversation, it wasn't necessarily meaningful to her. The rapport the two of you quickly achieved does not make her think of you as a special friend, and having an intimate conversation does not commit her to future closeness.

C She has so many intimate conversations that she has forgotten all about this one.

Comments

B is the most probable answer. You'll have to build up more of a shared history before you become anybody special to her. Why don't you call her? This may prove to be a real friendship some day; it just isn't one yet. C is a possibility as well.

SITUATION FIVE

A friend is visiting your house when the phone rings. It is someone you don't hear from often and you are anxious to catch up on their news. What should you do?

A Ignore the visiting friend in favour of the telephoning one and have a nice, long chat. Apologize when you hang up.

B Express your happiness at hearing from the caller, then explain that you have company and ask when you can return the call.

C You shouldn't have answered the phone at all.

Comments

Either *B* or *C*. Not answering the phone is easier if you have an answering machine. A live visitor should always take precedence over the one who dropped in by phone. As Americans allocate their time carefully, they will resent their visiting time with you being idled away while you talk to someone else. Even if there are other people around to entertain, guests will not like being treated as second fiddles.

SITUATION SIX

While visiting the USA on business you would like to make contact with Company X. How do you go about it?

A Find out who is in charge of your area of interest and write to him or her well in advance of your visit. Suggest what you might do for Company X. If the response is positive, set up a precise appointment before leaving home.

B Step in at Company X's office during the course of your visit and ask to see the president.

C Call a day or two in advance and make a date to visit with anyone who's around.

Comments

A is best. As Americans hate to waste time, they're not apt to see you unless they have good reason to believe it's worthwhile. You can chance *C* sometimes, but your odds are poor of seeing anyone consequential. *B* is fairly hopeless, although out of politeness some minor functionary may see you. As a person with demonstrated time to spend in waiting, you will be assumed to be of little importance.

SITUATION SEVEN

You hire a nanny. Although you consider her wages very high, you are glad to have her as she is sensible and reliable. However, it distresses you that she calls you by your first name. You don't want to hurt her feelings, but you wish she would call you Mrs. Ayashi. Can you ask her to?

A No. She would be too insulted at the suggestion. She hasn't called anyone by their title since her schooldays.

B Yes, but you must ask tactfully.

C Yes, just tell her you think it is very rude of her to call you by first name.

Comments

B. Tact should spare hurt feelings. You might bring up the subject at a happy moment when you are offering some kind of treat so that she will realize that you bear her no ill will personally.

If she is a mature woman, we assume that you have taken care to call her Mrs. XX, rather than by her first name. You should explain to her that in your country only people who have known each other for a very long time are on first name terms, and while you hold her in high regard, you cannot get used to the sound of your given name coming from someone you met so recently. You might add that you know this is not the custom in the USA and you understand that she does not mean to be rude. If she is a great deal younger than you, you may call her by her first name while explaining that where you come from younger people always address older ones by their title.

DOS AND DON'TS APPENDIX

DO wear dress-up clothes to a funeral.

DO keep track of your place in line at the cash register when shopping. Even if the line is invisible, everyone will know who is first, next, and so on.

DO use the Internet at public libraries if you don't have an Internet service at home.

DO help with the housework, even if you're a man. Americans think men who don't are being unfair. Your wife will come to believe this too.

DO thank hosts who have entertained you by calling, e-mailing, or sending a note.

DO send or bring a present if good friends have a new baby. The present might be a meal for the family.

DO encourage your children to go to college even if they aren't academically inclined. College is very important in the USA.

DO have a shower or bath every day.

DO ask if it's all right to smoke before you light up, wherever you are.

DO shave your underarms and legs below the knees (for women), if you want to Americanize.

DO say "God bless you" or "gesundheit" when someone sneezes. It's an old custom that is supposed to keep vital forces from escaping.

DO go see a therapist if you feel very depressed, anxious, or distraught. It doesn't mean you're crazy, and therapists have techniques that are very helpful.

DO ask questions if you're unsure or confused about anything. People will be happy to help you.

DO arrive 10–15 minutes late to a dinner party.

DO make reservations at busy restaurants by calling first.

DO say "no ice" if you don't want it; otherwise your drinks will come with it.

DO try to learn something about the rules of football and the name of the local team. Whether they win or lose is a great source of conversation.

DO pay your traffic and parking tickets.

DO take time to rest when you can. Just being in a foreign culture and remembering all the different ways of doing things is tiring.

DO NOT try to bribe police or other officials.

DO NOT arrive late for a wedding.

DO NOT yawn, if you can help it, as yawning indicates boredom. If you must yawn, cover your mouth.

DO NOT stick out your tongue at anyone.

DO NOT expect your children to support you in your old age.

DO NOT be hurt if your children want to leave home when they're 18. For American children, it's natural.

DO NOT spend too much time watching television or cruising the Internet. These are addictions.

DO NOT buy illegal drugs from people on the street. That drug seller could be an undercover cop, and you could go to jail.

DO NOT hitchhike. It's not safe. And don't pick up hitchhikers either.

DO NOT change into your bathing suit on the beach.

DO NOT take your shoes off when you go in someone's house. And don't put your feet on the furniture either.

DO NOT make derogatory comments about ethnic or racial groups.

DO NOT ask people how much money they make or have or how much their new car or house cost.

DO NOT feel obligated to check your coat in restaurants or museums.

DO NOT snap your fingers to call a waiter.

DO NOT start eating at a meal until everyone has been served.

DO NOT tip customs officials, police, airline personnel, store clerks, room clerks, receptionists, or elevator operators. (*See* Resources *for who you* should *tip*.)

DO NOT be rude. Americans are straightforward but polite.

GLOSSARY

AA: Alcoholics Anonymous. A self-help program for alcoholics.

AIDS: Acquired Immune Deficiency Syndrome.

A/C: Air conditioning.

AM and PM: The AM hours are from midnight to noon; PM hours from noon to midnight. So, 3 PM is the middle of the afternoon, not the middle of the night. Americans rarely use the 24-hour clock.

ASAP: As soon as possible. Meaning, do it right away.

ATM: Automated Teller Machine, where you can make deposits and get cash. An ATM card is one that lets you access your bank account.

Black: The color of mourning; often worn at funerals.

CPS: Child Protective Services – the agency that will be called if someone suspects you're mistreating your children.

Class of 2007: In college, people are divided up according to the year they graduate (or are supposed to graduate). As college is supposed to take four years – although it often takes more these days – someone who starts college in September of 2003 would be referred to as "in the class of 2007." If he drops back a year, he would then become "the class of 2008."

Classifieds: Paid listings for jobs, etc., in newspapers or on the Internet.

c/o: care of; used when forwarding mail. Joe Smith c/o Jim Dandy.

College: An institution of higher learning that students attend after high school. A four-year course may earn a student a B.A. (Bachelor of Arts) or a B.S. (Bachelor of Science).

Cop: Policeman or policewoman.

Cruelty-free: Products that do not use animal products and are produced without being tested on animals.

DDT: A pesticide that had deadly effects on the environment. It's now illegal, but residues remain.

First floor: In the USA, the first floor is the ground or street-level floor. The second floor is one flight up.

Funeral: A service following a death, at which the body is present in a coffin. In a *memorial service* the body is not present, although the ashes may be.

Green Card: The document allowing a foreigner to live and work in the USA.

High school: The last four years of school, grades 9 through 12, when students are usually 14–18 years old. Junior high school is the two or three years before high school; elementary school comprises the first five or six grades, which children start at age six.

ICU: Intensive Care Unit – where the most critically ill people in a hospital are cared for.

ID: Identification, such as a driver's license or passport.

INS: Immigration and Naturalisation Service, the agency that controls who comes and goes from the USA.

IRS: Internal Revenue Service, the agency that collects federal taxes.

K-12: Kindergarten through 12th grade.

Medicare: Government-paid health insurance that nearly all Americans and legal residents over 65 qualify for.

Ms.: Form of address for women, married or not. It's particularly useful for letters, e.g. "Dear Ms. Rice."

Pharmacy: Place to buy prescription drugs, as well as toiletries, and sometimes nearly everything you might want. Also called "drug stores" but not "chemists."

R & D: Research and Development – a department in some companies, usually where new products are developed.

R & R: Rest and relaxation. As in "I'm planning some R & R this weekend."

Rest rooms: The polite way to ask for the toilet. You can also ask for a bathroom when what you really want is the toilet. You can also say "ladies' room" or "men's room."

"Right to bear arms": The phrase from the US constitution that gun supporters think justifies them in insisting that guns should be legal.

Sept. 11: The day in 2001 when terrorists attacked the World Trade Center and the Pentagon (Defense Dept. headquarters). It is often referred to now without explanation, as in "Since 9/11, people have been more insecure."

Social Security: The pension that most workers get from the government, currently at age 65.

SSN: Social Security Number. All working citizens and residents have one. If you're not eligible for a SSN, you can get a Tax Payer ID, which enables you to open a bank account.

Strike out: A baseball term meaning to fail.

Toll-free numbers: If instead of an area code, a phone number has the prefix 800, 888, 877, or 866, the call won't cost you anything. The most common toll-free number is 800; the other numbers were added recently because the 800 numbers were all taken. A 900 number, on the other hand, indicates a very high-priced call.

24/7: Twenty-four hours a day, seven days a week, i.e. all the time. As in, "I've been working 24/7."

Uncle Sam: The US government. For example, "Uncle Sam takes a lot of my money."

University: An institution of higher learning that includes a four-year college, as well as advanced schools of study (graduate schools).

Vegan: A vegetarian does not eat meat; a vegan does not eat meat, fish, or dairy products.

X: The symbol of a kiss, which you might use in signing a letter. Also used by teachers to indicate an answer is wrong.

X-rated: Pornographic.

Zip code: The five-number suffix used in all US addresses. Properly, a four-number code follows the zip code, narrowing down the location still further.

CALENDAR OF HOLIDAYS

The USA has 10 federal holidays observed countrywide. Four are set by date:

New Year's Day — January 1
Independence Day — July 4
Veterans Day — November 11
Christmas Day — December 25

If any of the above fall on a Saturday, then Friday is usually observed as a holiday. Similarly, if one falls on a Sunday, then Monday is usually the holiday.

The other six holidays are set by a day of the week and the month:

Martin Luther King's Birthday — Third Monday in January
Washington's Birthday — Third Monday in February
Memorial Day — Last Monday in May
Labor Day — First Monday in September
Columbus Day — Second Monday in October
Thanksgiving — Fourth Thursday in November

See pages 179–186 for a description of these holidays and other US celebrations observed throughout the year.

RESOURCE GUIDE

Anything.com
A website that has references to excellent sites for everything from airlines, credit cards, and travel to medicine, cooking, and maps.

Buses
Usually the cheapest way to get around. Greyhound (800-229-9424; **www.greyhound.com**) crisscrosses the country. Trailways is an association of regional bus lines with separate phone numbers, which you can find at **www.trailways.com**

Disabilities
Thanks to the American Disabilities Act, facilities for the handicapped are good. Public places are supposed to provide access and rest room facilities for people in wheelchairs. However, older systems of public transportation (like the New York subway system) predate modern construction standards. City streets usually have ramps at curbs. You must not leave your car in such a way as to impede wheelchair crossings.

If you're traveling in a wheelchair, you will find a lot of help from *The Traveler's Guide To Wheelchairs*. A useful website for travelers with disabilities is **www.projectaction.org**

Drinking
Rules for sale of alcohol vary from state to state and county to county. Some places are altogether "dry," i.e. no alcohol is sold. Generally, you can buy wine and beer more freely than stronger liquor, but you must be 21 years old to buy it.

You can get in a lot of trouble if you are picked up driving with a high blood alcohol level, which roughly speaking means more than a couple of small drinks in a couple of hours. You are also not to have an open bottle or can of alcohol in your car.

Driving

Auto insurance: Most states require it in order to register a car, which you must do at the state Department of Motor Vehicles. You'll want to shop around for a policy and decide how much insurance you want. It is also useful to join AAA, which provides road service when you break down, as well as maps, guidebooks, and trip planning advice. AAA also sells automobile insurance, as do many other companies.

Drivers' licenses: Drivers from most countries can use their home driver's licenses in the USA for up to a year. An International Driving Permit is useful for drivers whose licenses don't have a photo on them, particularly young-looking people needing to prove they are old enough to buy alcohol and go to nightclubs.

Gas: Most gas stations are self-serve. You will have to get out of the car, pay at the pump with a credit card or inside the station with cash or credit, and then follow directions to fill the gas tank yourself. You will also have to wash your own car windows and add oil, air, and water yourself. A few gas stations still have islands labeled full serve; gas prices are higher at these.

Parking: When you're parking on a street, look around for signs announcing parking hours. Curb colour has meaning: Red – no parking; Blue – handicapped only; White – unloading only; Green – very short-term parking. You car can be towed away if you park illegally, and you will find getting it back most inconvenient.

Rental cars: Drivers are usually required to be 25 years of age, though some companies will allow 21–25-year-olds to rent with an additional charge. You also need a valid driver's license and a credit card. The rental company will try and sell you accident insurance; you may be covered through home insurance or even a credit card, but unless you are sure of this, buy the additional insurance.

Emergencies

911 is the emergency number nearly everywhere in the USA. This will bring you police, the fire department, or an ambulance.

Entry Requirements

Customs: When entering the USA, you may bring in 1 liter of alcohol, 100 cigars, and 200 cigarettes without paying duties. You may bring in bakery items and certain cheeses but not meat or meat products, fruit, or vegetables.

Pet dogs and cats may be brought into the USA, subject to health inspection; dogs coming from a country not free of rabies must have a rabies vaccination certificate issued at least 30 days before departure. Individual airlines may require health certificates.

You may bring in a generous number of household items for your own use and gifts of up to $100 in value. Do not bring in firearms unless they're for hunting; these you must take with you when you leave. All drugs must be clearly labeled, in reasonable quantity, and accompanied by a prescription or doctor's statement that you require them. If you bring in more than $10,000 in cash, money orders or traveler's checks, you must file a report with customs.

For further details, see **www.customs.ustreas.gov**

Immigration: **www.ins.gov** will lead you to the source for application forms and answers to many questions. The American Immigration Center at **www.us-immigration.com** (800-814-1555 or from outside the country call 505-891-1555) provides information and sells do-it-yourself kits for processing your own applications.

Passports: All nationalities except Canadians and Mexicans need passports to enter the USA. If you lose yours, notify both the police and your home embassy.

Visas: Under the recent Visa Waiver Program, people from certain countries can enter the USA for business or pleasure for up to 90 days without a visa. You must come on an airline that belongs to the program. Visas are generally available for people who want to stay for up to six months as tourists or visitors; it is a great deal harder to get a visa that will allow you to work here. Students must be accepted by a American school before applying for a student visa. In all, there are some 40 different kinds of visas; you should apply in the US consulate of your home country before you depart. It is possible to change your visa status after you arrive by applying to the INS. New strictures have been added since 9/11, particularly for people from countries that "harbor terrorists." It is now extra-important for be sure that all your papers are exactly in order.

For information: **http://travel.state.gov/visa_services.html**

Gambling

Gambling is only allowed in select places, such as Atlantic City and Nevada, which includes Las Vegas, and on Indian reservations, which escape state laws. State lotteries are further exceptions to laws against gambling, as is racetrack betting.

Health

Dental clinics: private dentists do almost all dentistry. The larger cities have dentistry schools that run low-cost clinics, but the process of being treated by them is lengthy.

Dental Insurance: Much less common than medical insurance, which 15% of Americans lack.

Fluoride: Most of the tap water has added fluoride, which has greatly reduced cavities among children.

Health insurance: For stays under six months in the USA, buy travel insurance from a company in your home country (a travel agent can help you). If you're getting a job in the USA, be sure your employer will provide health insurance. If you do not have insurance through an employer, school, or other family member, you will have to purchase it. There are numerous companies. The largest is Blue Cross/Blue Shield at **www.bluecares.com**; 800-333-0912.

Health threats: The threat of disease in the USA is no greater than in any other developed nation, despite increasing tuberculosis, seasonal outbreaks of flu, and outbreaks of West Nile Virus around New York City. Food-borne diseases originating in meat, such as E Coli 057 and salmonellosis have increased

Nature presents some threats. Mosquitoes, which are worst at dawn and dusk, are bothersome but not dangerous. Ticks, unfortunately, can carry Lyme disease – a chronic debilitating condition. Lyme Disease is endemic in the Northeast and upper Midwest; lolling in the grass on a summer's day in those areas is not as carefree as it once was. You now want to wear shoes and socks and inspect your body for ticks daily – ticks bite you and hang on. If you remove them within 24 hours you should be okay. If you're going into the woods, get somebody to identify poison ivy and poison oak for you. Both can cause horrible, itchy rashes. Learn about rattlesnakes before you go hiking in the West. More information available at: **www.cdc.gov/travel**

Take the proper precautions regarding sexually transmitted diseases here as everywhere in the world. Not only must you beware of HIV but Hepatitis C is rampant, as are various infections.

HMO: Health Maintenance Organization. A group that provides complete health care to its members. People who belong to an HMO are discouraged from using doctors outside the HMO's own providers. The advantage is that HMOs are cheaper than plans that allow you free choice of doctors.

md.com: Leads you to websites that enable you to buy drugs cheaply.

PPO: Preferred Provider Organization. A method of insurance that limits members to seeing only the doctors that are enrolled in its plan.

Vaccinations: No vaccines are specifically required to enter the USA, but if you're planning to stay, you ought to see a physician and discuss vaccines you might need. It helps if you have brought your medical records from home.

Before starting school, children must have proof of immunisation against diphtheria, measles, polio, rubella, tetanus, pertussis, mumps, and Hepatitis B (in some states).

House & Home
Buying a home: You'll find useful information on the website of the US Department of Housing and Urban Development at: **www.hud.gov**

Electricity: 110–120 volts AC, so European appliances generally need an adapter.

Garbage Collection: Nearly every community has some regular collection; sometimes the city pays, sometimes you do.

Moving: There are numerous companies that come to your house, pick up your things, and take them to your new house – or to storage. If you are making a major move, you might want to get several price quotes before choosing a company. Be wary of unknown companies quoting ultra-low bids. They have been known to hold people's goods hostage for additional payments.

Telephone: To have one installed, call your local phone company and make arrangements. Because long-distance companies have been deregulated in recent years, you will have to select the carrier you want. It probably won't make much difference which one you choose, but you may want to consider one that gives you low rates for international calls. A cheap alternative for international calls is to dial 1016868-011, followed by country code and number.

Legal Matters
www.nolo.com is a great fount of legal information, on everything from probate to divorce to Internet law to small claims court.

Lost & Found
Each company, whether bus, train, taxi company, airline, hotel, theatre, restaurant or other public place, has its own system for holding lost property. Contact them if you lose something. Your chances of getting it back are quite good. You can also try the police.

Mail
Post offices are usually open from 9-5, though large ones may have self-service sections that are open longer hours. You can have mail sent to you c/o General Delivery at the main post office of whatever city or town you are in; you will need to pick it up personally. Letters should all include the five-figure zip code. Delivery takes one to three days within the continental USA. As of this writing, the domestic rate for a one-ounce letter is 37¢. Each additional ounce is 23¢. Postcards are 23¢. Package rate varies according to distance. Domestic (books and tapes) media mail is a great bargain at $1.33 per pound and 45¢ for each additional pound. Express mail is expensive but promises overnight delivery. Most international letters (up to 1 ounce) are 80¢. For precise details see: **www.usps.com**

A number of private mail handlers have sprung up, with names such as Mail Boxes Etc. and Postal Plus. These charge extra for their services but are fast. They will wrap your packages as well as ship them; they generally also have copiers available, provide fax services, and provide FedEx shipment.

Envelopes: How to address:

Your Name
Your Street Address
Your City, State, Zip Code

STAMP

Recipient's Name
Company's Name
Street Address
City, State, Zip Code
Country (if outside the USA)

Measures

Despite attempts, the USA still hasn't made the switch to the metric system. The following are rough equivalencies.

Americans measure weights in ounces and pounds. There are 16 ounces in a pound. 1 ounce=28 grams. 1 pound is about 1/2 a kilogram or 500 grams. 1 kilogram=2.2 pounds.

Lengths are in inches, feet and yards. There are 12 inches in a foot and 3 feet in a yard. An inch=2.5 centimeters. One meter=3.2 feet. One meter=1.09 of a yard.

Distances are measured in miles. 1 mile=1.6 kilometers.

In cooking, Americans measure rather than weigh. Both liquids and dry foods are measured in teaspoons, tablespoons, cups, pints, quarts, and gallons. 3 teaspoons=1 tablespoon. 16 tablespoons=1 cup. There are 2 cups in a pint, 2 pints in a quart, and 4 quarts in a gallon. A liter is slightly more than a quart. 1 gallon=3.8 liters.

Temperatures are measured in Fahrenheit rather than Celsius. To change Fahrenheit into Centigrade subtract 32 and divide by 1.8. Freezing point is 32 degrees in Fahrenheit and boiling point is 212° F.

Money

Currency: American bills come all in the same size and colour, so look carefully before you part with them. You will see $1s, $2s (extremely rare), $5s, $10s, $20s, $50s, and $100s. Coins come in a 1 (penny), 5 (nickel), 10 (dime), 25 (quarter), and, rarely, 1 dollar. There is little relationship between the coin's size and its value, so watch carefully here too.

Exchanging money: Credit cards provide a good and up-to-date exchange rate. Most ATM machines take the Star and the Cirrius networks. If you plan to withdraw money from a credit card account, be sure you have your four-digit PIN with you.

Income Taxes: The federal tax is the largest. It is a sliding scale according to income; the highest rate (income of above $307,050) currently is 38.6%. Some states also have income taxes, but they are much lower than the federal tax. There is also a social security tax that takes 15.3% of up to $87,000 from a paycheck and pays for retirement and health care of those aged 65 and over. Americans generally hate taxes even more than people in other countries. President George W. Bush ran for president promising to "give your money back to you."

Sales tax: A tax added on to every purchase is a primary way that states and localities collect revenue. The amount, from 4–8%, varies from place to place, and a few states have none. If you are having something mailed to a location outside of the sales tax region of the store where you bought it, you needn't pay the sales tax. Groceries are rarely taxed.

Police

Policing responsibilities are divided among state, county, and city forces. There is no national police force other than the FBI (Federal Bureau of Investigation), which concentrates on major interstate crimes. You are only likely to meet the state police if you speed on a state highway. County governments have sheriffs' departments, and if you are robbed you will deal with them or the local city police force.

Radio
Radio frequencies are divided into AM and FM. The classier stations – National Public Radio, classical music – are nearly all on FM.

Services
Childcare: Agencies are listed under "child care" or "babysitting" in the yellow pages. If you don't have a personal recommendation, it is best to ask for references and to check them.

Housecleaners: The usual way to find help is through newspaper advertisements, though there are a great variety of cleaning services listed in the yellow pages of any city. You don't need a license to open a cleaning service, so you should try and get a recommendation.

Smoking
Foreigners are frequently put out by the hostile attitude toward smoking in the USA. We simply consider other countries backward to allow smokers to freely pollute the air.

The laws vary greatly both by state and by town. California, Delaware, and New York City have laws barring smoking in any public place, including restaurants and bars. In many cities, restaurants don't allow smoking or have nonsmoking sections. Other states have few laws against smoking. You must be at least 18 to buy cigarettes, and even older in a few states. For the etiquette of smoking in private homes, see pages 103–104.

Store hours
They vary widely. Some department stores are open 10 a.m. to 9 p.m. every weekday, closing at 6 p.m. on weekends. Others normally

close at 6:30 p.m., except on Thursdays, when they stay open until 9 p.m. Some supermarkets are open 24-hours a day. Many drugstores close at 9 p.m, others at midnight.

In some communities, everything closes early. Smaller specialty stores may be closed on Sundays, especially if they are located in business districts.

Telephone

Numbers: All numbers have first a three-number area code, followed by seven numbers. Generally, you do not have to dial the area code if you are calling someone within the same area code.

Calling: Pay phones cost 35¢ to 50¢ a minute for local locals; long-distance calls are much higher. You can save money by buying *phone cards* instead. Or you may want to get a *cell phone* for your stay. If you do not want to sign a year's contract, you can buy a new or refurbished cell phone from a wireless phone company (AT&T does this) and rather than signing a contract, you can buy prepaid phone cards for your calls. Prices vary from about 12¢ to 35¢ a minute. You can also rent cell phones from cellular/satellite phone rental companies, but the rates are exorbitant. Sprint will rent you a phone on a monthly basis. It costs $10 more a month than with a yearly contract. Plans start at around $40 a month.

Hotel calls: Charges for calls from a hotel room phone are generally very high. Inquire before you make any.

Information: To get a local phone number, call 411. For another area code, dial the code and 555-1212. The charge for information is usually $1.50. Telephone directories are often divided into residential and personal sections; there is then another section (or in large cities, another book) called the Yellow Pages, which lists services and vendors alphabetically. A local phone book is always excellent reading, full of useful information.

Television: Before cable television, all TV stations were broadcast over the airwaves. Some still are, and these are the giants on your TV dial: ABC, CBS, NBC, and Fox. But these days, they get a lot of competition from cable stations. These stations require you to pay for a cable hookup, but are not available everywhere. PBS (Public Broadcasting Service) is found on both network and cable; this is the publicly supported channel that has few ads and more uplifting programming than the usual fare.

Tipping
Airport:
　　Electric cart transport: $1–$2
　　Skycap: $1 per bag (transport or curbside check-in)
　　Wheelchair assistance: $3–$5
Barber or beautician: 10–15%
Casino:
　　Dealer: $5–$100 when you leave. If you win a jackpot, tip everyone in sight lavishly, including the security guard.
Coat check: $1
Hotel:
　　Bellhop: $5 for taking you to your room
　　Chambermaid: $1–$2 per night
　　Doorman: $1 for hailing a cab
　　Flowers delivery: $2–$5
　　Hotel room service: 10–15% of bill
　　Restaurants: $2–$10.
Manicurist: $2–$5
Masseuse: 10%
Movers: $10–$50
Parking garage attendant: $1
Pizza Delivery: $1–$5 depending on distance

Restaurant:
    Counter server: 10%
    Waiter: 15–20%
Rest room attendant: 50¢–$1
Shampoo person: $1–$2.
Taxi drivers: 10% of bill
Tour bus driver: $1–$2
Tour guide: 10–15% of tour cost
Tow truck operator: $3–$5
Ushers: Do not tip
Valet parking: $2–$5

Time
Continental USA has four time zones. The East Coast is three hours ahead of the West Coast.

Travel
Budget Accommodations: In major cities, you can usually find reasonably priced lodgings in a YMCA or YWCA. There are also many hostels sponsored by Hostelling International–American Youth Hostels (**www.hiayh.org**) across the United States. These can be pleasant and sociable, but you won't get much more than a bunk. For budget hotels, there are numerous guidebooks, such as *Let's Go USA*. There are also hotel brokers that discount empty rooms at very large savings if business is slow. 800-USA-HOTEL (800-872-4683; **www.1800usahotels.com**) has nationwide service, as does Quikbook (800-789-9887; **www. quikbook.com**). Central Reservation Service specialises in Boston, Orlando and San Francisco: 407-740-6442 from within the United States and 1-800-894-0680 from overseas; **www.roomconnection.com**.

Directions: **www.mapquest.com** is a remarkable website that delivers precise directions to almost anywhere.

Flying: Since the attacks on September 11, 2001, the restrictions on carry-on luggage have become much tighter. Do not try to take on board the plane with you: metal nail files or clippers, scissors, knives, box cutters, or anything else that could conceivably be used as a weapon.

Trains: Amtrak is the national railroad company, and you can travel from the Atlantic to the Pacific on it in comfort, or speed up and down either coast on Amtrak trains. Amtrak offers 15- and 30-day passes with unlimited stopovers for foreigners at attractive prices. Call 800-USA-RAIL or see: **www.amtrak.com**

Water
The tap water everywhere is considered quite safe to drink, although many people buy water, which they consider purer and better tasting.

Weather
www.worldclimate.com gives you average temperatures and rainfall; **www.nws.noaa.gov** gives you current conditions and forecasts.

FURTHER READING

The following recommendations include only those books that I feel would be most helpful to foreigners trying to understand Americans and their way of life. It is, of course, far from a complete reading list.

American Cultural Patterns. Edward C. Stewart, Intercultural Press, 1972. An excellent study of American beliefs and behavior.

American Ways. Gary Althen, Intercultural Press, 2002. An easy-to-read and thorough review of American attitudes and customs by a foreign student advisor. A new, updated edition.

Bowling Alone: The Collapse and Revival of American Community. Robert D. Putnam. Simon & Schuster, 2000. A wealth of active civic organizations were a strong force in America's success. Putnam, a Harvard sociologist, demonstrates the decline of "social capital" in the last 30 years and pleads for a revival, saying that social connectedness is better than Prozac for what ails us.

Catfish and Mandala. Andrew X. Pham. Farrar, Straus and Giroux, 1999. While bicycling through the land of his birth, Vietnam, Pham reflects on his adopted country: "But now, I miss the white, the black, the red, the brown faces of America...their idealistic search for racial equality, their bumbling but wonderful pioneering spirit."

The Century. Peter Jennings and Todd Brewster, Doubleday, 1998. A large pictorial history of the US in the 20th century, with eyewitness accounts of eras and events. Very readable.

Class. Paul Fussell, Ballantine Publishing, 1983. Not only does Fussell insist that America has a class system, he describes in minute detail the elements that separate the strata. A most amusing book and thoroughly practical for anyone who seriously wishes to rise socially.

Cultural Misunderstandings. Raymonde Carroll. The University Chicago Press, 1988. If you're just going to read one book on cultural differences, this is the one. Compares French and Americans, but the points are universal.

Dance of Life. Edward T. Hall, Anchor Books/Doubleday, 1983. An anthropologist explains why time is perceived so differently in various cultures and why Americans go by the clock.

Democracy in America. Alexis de Tocqueville, NAL, 1991 (first published in 1835). De Tocqueville wrote about the uniqueness of America, and many of his observations remain apt today.

Domestic Manners of the Americans. Fanny Trollope, Oxford University Press, 1984 (first published in 1832). Mrs. Trollope, a lively writer, found Americans ignorant and parties dull, but she grants that the USA was a fine country to get ahead in.

Future Shock. Alvin Toffler, Random House, 1970. Describes how a fast-changing world affects personal stability and communities.

Host Family Survival Kit. Nancy King and Ken Huff, Intercultural Press, 1997. A guide for Americans who are sheltering exchange students, but equally useful in helping the students understand the hosts. Includes a good description of the culture shock process.

In Search of Self in India and Japan: Toward a Cross-Cultural Psychology. Alan Roland, Princeton University Press, 1988. A psychoanalyst who worked with American, Japanese, and Indian patients discovers very basic differences in family attachments.

Living and Working in America: A Survival Handbook. David Hampshire, Survival Books, 1998. A thick, detailed book full of specifics on everything from highway driving to shoe sizes. The breezy, frank style makes it as interesting as it is useful.

Lost in Translation. Eva Hoffman, E. P. Dutton, 1989. A beautifully written account of life in America by a Polish-born refugee.

The New Dictionary of Cultural Literacy: What Every American Needs to Know. E.D. Hirsch, Jr., Joseph Kett and James Trefil. Houghton Mifflin, 2002. A very handy roundup of all the basic information that Americans share – including a who's who in the Bible, common sayings and idioms, and famous people, dates, and quotes from literature.

People of Plenty: Economic Abundance and the American Character. David M. Potter, University of Chicago Press, 1954. Recognizes how much of American behavior is simply an outgrowth of affluence.

People's History of the United States. Howard Zinn, Perennial, 2001. History from the point of view of the poor and powerless.

"What We Think of America": *Granta 77,* April 2002 issue, London. Edited by Ian Jack. Perspectives on America in the post 9/11 era by distinguished writers from Lebanon, India, Serbia, the Middle East, Europe, Chile, China, Canada, Australia, Turkey, and Malaysia.

What's So Great About America. Dinesh D'Souza. Regnery Publishing, 2002. D'Souza, an immigrant from India, sees problems in American life, but thinks the freedom and tolerance still make it great. What's more, he points out, to people from places where the poor starve, the appeal of a country where the poor people are fat is obvious.

THE AUTHOR

Esther Wanning was born in Boston, Massachusetts, and is descended from New England Yankees on both sides of her family. She grew up in a rural setting but spent her young adulthood in New York City, where she worked as a magazine and travel book editor. After a short stint as a teacher, she moved to San Francisco to marry her husband, who is of Jewish Hungarian and Russian descent. She now lives in Marin County, California.

She has written for numerous publications and, in addition to *Culture Shock! USA*, is the author of *Surviving Without Cigarettes* and *The Art of Maryland*. In true American fashion, she returned to school in midlife and earned a master's degree in counseling psychology. While continuing to write, she now also works as a therapist.

INDEX